Forecasting
Religious Affiliation
in the United
States Army

MELISSA HALLER

Prepared for the United States Army
Approved for public release; distribution unlimited

 ARROYO CENTER

For more information on this publication, visit **www.rand.org/t/RRA752-2**.

About RAND

The RAND Corporation is a research organization that develops solutions to public policy challenges to help make communities throughout the world safer and more secure, healthier and more prosperous. RAND is nonprofit, nonpartisan, and committed to the public interest. To learn more about RAND, visit www.rand.org.

Research Integrity

Our mission to help improve policy and decisionmaking through research and analysis is enabled through our core values of quality and objectivity and our unwavering commitment to the highest level of integrity and ethical behavior. To help ensure our research and analysis are rigorous, objective, and nonpartisan, we subject our research publications to a robust and exacting quality-assurance process; avoid both the appearance and reality of financial and other conflicts of interest through staff training, project screening, and a policy of mandatory disclosure; and pursue transparency in our research engagements through our commitment to the open publication of our research findings and recommendations, disclosure of the source of funding of published research, and policies to ensure intellectual independence. For more information, visit www.rand.org/about/principles.

RAND's publications do not necessarily reflect the opinions of its research clients and sponsors.

Published by the RAND Corporation, Santa Monica, Calif.
© 2021 RAND Corporation
RAND® is a registered trademark.

Library of Congress Cataloging-in-Publication Data is available for this publication.

ISBN: 978-1-9774-0736-8

Cover: Alamy Stock Photo.

About This Report

This report documents research and analysis conducted as part of a project entitled *Army Chaplain Corps Strategic Plan*, sponsored by the Office of the Chief of Chaplains (OCCH). The purpose of the project was to assist in development of a long-term strategic plan for the Chaplain's branch of the U.S. Army, which will include operational mission area assignments, personnel life cycle goals, leader development plans, and program management assessment processes.

This research was conducted within RAND Arroyo Center's Personnel, Training, and Health Program. RAND Arroyo Center, part of the RAND Corporation, is a federally funded research and development center (FFRDC) sponsored by the United States Army.

RAND operates under a "Federal-Wide Assurance" (FWA00003425) and complies with the *Code of Federal Regulations for the Protection of Human Subjects Under United States Law* (45 CFR 46), also known as "the Common Rule," as well as with the implementation guidance set forth in the U.S Department of Defense (DoD) Instruction 3216.02. As applicable, this compliance includes reviews and approvals by RAND's Institutional Review Board (the Human Subjects Protection Committee) and by the U.S. Army. The views of sources utilized in this study are solely their own and do not represent the official policy or position of DoD or the U.S. Government.

Contents

Figures and Tables

Figures

Tables

Summary

The U.S. Army's Office of the Chief of Chaplains (OCCH) requested that RAND Arroyo Center examine U.S. demographic trends in religious affiliation. As the religious composition of the United States changes, not only does it impact the religious composition of recruits, but it also has the potential to significantly change the religious needs of the Army population for years to come. To prepare for these changes, OCCH will need to consider changes to the U.S. Army Chaplain Corps's (DACH's) force mix, to both monitor and adjust that mix over time.

To examine these demographic trends, the research team analyzed administrative data on enlisted soldiers, chaplains, and officers in the Regular Army (RA), as well as data from a nationally representative survey of the U.S. population, the General Social Survey (GSS), to answer the following questions:

- How has the religious composition of enlisted RA soldiers changed over time?
- How does the religious composition of the U.S. population compare with the religious composition of the enlisted RA?
- How does the religious composition of RA chaplains compare with the religious composition of enlisted RA soldiers?
- What is the likely projected religious composition of the enlisted RA over the next five years?
- How might these projections change if the Army increases recruitment from currently underrepresented regions of the United States?

- How has the religious composition of RA officers changed over time?
- What is the likely projected religious composition of RA officers over the next five years?
- What can we learn about the potential spiritual needs of individuals who report not having a religious affiliation?

To study religious trends, we examined the total and relative proportions of the Army population in broad religious categories as defined by the GSS, and we further analyzed these trends by detailed religious family groups as defined by the Association of Religious Data Archives (ARDA). We made five-year forecasts for the largest religious groups among enlisted soldiers and officers in the RA, incorporating information on current and potential shifts in geographic recruitment patterns.

What We Found

How Has the Religious Composition of Enlisted Regular Army Soldiers Changed over Time?

The three largest groups in the enlisted RA are Protestants, Catholics, and those who report having no religious preference, are atheists, or are agnostics; these last three categories are referred to throughout the report collectively as "Nones" and do not include enlisted soldiers for whom we do not have any information about religious affiliation. The proportion of Protestants increased from fiscal year (FY) 2000 to FY 2015, and after FY 2015 it began to decline modestly, while the proportion of Catholics has declined steadily since FY 2005. The proportion of "Nones" fell between FY 2000 and FY 2015 but has since increased.[1] These patterns are largely driven by the religious composition of soldiers coming from the southern United States, who make up nearly half of enlisted soldiers. Breaking down these broad religious groups

---

[1] Between FY 2007 and FY 2015, the increase in the share of Protestants coincided with a decrease in the number of enlisted soldiers for whom we do not have any information about religious affiliation.

further into denominational families, we find that, within Protestants, the share of enlisted soldiers who identify as "nondenominational Protestant" is growing substantially, while the shares who identify with most other denominational families have declined in recent years.

How Does the Religious Composition of the U.S. Population Compare with the Religious Composition of the Enlisted Regular Army?

Comparing the enlisted RA to U.S. population, we find that while Protestants are the largest group overall in both populations, the proportion of Protestants is increasing in the RA but is decreasing in the United States as a whole. The United States also has a larger proportion of Catholics than the RA does. While the RA initially had a larger proportion of "Nones," the proportion of "Nones" in the U.S. population has grown rapidly in the past 20 years and is approximately equivalent to the current proportion in the RA. We also compare the enlisted RA population to the population in the GSS with the same age, gender, and regional composition (which roughly approximates the youth cohort from the same regions of the country as RA personnel); this weighted transformation shows that the RA population is different from the broader population from which it is recruited. Based on the GSS data, we would expect the RA to have fewer Protestants, more Catholics, and more individuals in the "None" category than there are currently.

How Does the Religious Composition of Regular Army Chaplains Compare with the Religious Composition of Enlisted Regular Army Soldiers?

The top two religious groups represented by RA chaplains are Protestants and Catholics. There are approximately six Protestant chaplains for every 1,000 Protestant soldiers, and approximately one Catholic chaplain for every 1,000 Catholic soldiers. There also are considerable differences in the representation of religious families among the chaplains as compared with the composition of religious families among soldiers. These differences may be driven by the increasing tendency of soldiers to not identify with a particular Protestant denomination, but may reflect a true mismatch between the forms of Protestantism most common among the RA (possibly unaffiliated Christianity) and the ranks of DACH (Mainline Protestants).

What Is the Likely Projected Religious Composition of the Enlisted Regular Army over the Next Five Years?

Based on the current geographic makeup of the enlisted RA, our projections suggest that the proportions of Protestants and Catholics will likely decline modestly over time, while the proportion of "Nones" will likely increase.

How Might These Projections Change If the Army Increases Recruitment from Currently Underrepresented Regions of the United States?

We answer this question using two different scenarios: In one scenario, we assume that the Army shifts its geographic recruitment patterns but that this does not cause any religious groups to become more or less likely to enlist. We predict that this would cause a slight decrease in Protestants, relative to the status quo, and a slight increase in Catholics and "Nones." The second scenario assumes that shifting geographic recruitment patterns induce the religious composition of the Army to become more similar to the religious composition of the United States. In this scenario, there is a much larger decline in the population of Protestants, and a much larger increase in "Nones." The Catholic population increases substantially at first but declines over time.

How Has the Religious Composition of Regular Army Officers Changed over Time? What Is the Likely Projected Religious Composition of Regular Army Officers over the Next Five Years?

Officers in the Army tend to be considerably more religious than the enlisted population, with the "None" population making up about one-quarter of enlisted soldiers but less than 5 percent of RA officers. Based on trends in the data and our projections, we expect the religious composition of the officer population to remain relatively stable over the next five years compared with the composition of enlisted soldiers.

What Can We Learn About the Spiritual Needs of Individuals Who Report Not Having a Religious Affiliation?

We also investigate what the increase in the "None" population might mean for DACH. Using GSS data, we conclude that a sizeable proportion of individuals who identify in the "None" category (~83 percent) may still be somewhat spiritual (at minimum), while nearly 50 percent may be moderately or strongly spiritual. Based on this, we conclude that a large number of soldiers in the "None" category may still benefit from DACH services.

Acknowledgments

I am very grateful for the support I received from the RAND Corporation and RAND Arroyo Center as a summer associate, and am especially grateful to Shanthi Nataraj and Luke Matthews, who mentored me at RAND throughout the completion of this project. I would additionally like to thank Michael Hansen, Steve Dalzell, other members of the project team at RAND, the RAND Arroyo Center fellows for providing their support and insight, and Heather Krull for her helpful suggestions. I additionally want to thank Christine DeMartini and Beth Roth for their help with the more technical aspects of this project, and Tina Panis for all her assistance with the dataset and coding. Finally, I would like to thank Gina A. Zurlo, from the Center for the Study of Global Christianity at Gordon-Conwell Theological Seminary, and Julia Bandini, from RAND, for their tremendously helpful feedback and comments.

Abbreviations

ARDA	Association of Religion Data Archives
DACH	U.S. Army Chaplain Corps
FY	fiscal year
GSS	General Social Survey
NA	not available
OCCH	Office of the Chief of Chaplains
RA	Regular Army
RELTRAD	religious tradition
TAPDB	Total Army Personnel Database
TAPDB-AE	Total Army Personnel Database for Active Enlisted Soldiers
TAPDB-AO	Total Army Personnel Database for Active Officers

CHAPTER ONE

Introduction

The U.S. Army's Office of the Chief of Chaplains (OCCH) requested that the RAND Arroyo Center examine U.S. demographic trends in religious affiliation. As the religious composition of the United States changes, not only does this impact the religious composition of recruits, but it also has the potential to significantly change the religious needs of the Army population for years to come. To prepare for these changes, OCCH will need to consider changes to the U.S. Army Chaplain Corps's (DACH's) force mix, to both monitor and adjust that mix over time.

To examine these demographic trends, the research team analyzed administrative data on enlisted soldiers, chaplains, and officers in the Regular Army (RA) from the Total Army Personnel Database (TAPDB), as well as data from a nationally representative survey of the U.S. population, the General Social Survey (GSS), to investigate the following questions:

- How has the religious composition of enlisted RA soldiers changed over time?
- How does the religious composition of the U.S. population compare with the religious composition of the enlisted RA?
- How does the religious composition of RA chaplains compare with the religious composition of the enlisted RA?
- What is the likely projected religious composition of the enlisted RA over the next five years?
- How might these projections change if the Army increases recruitment from currently underrepresented regions of the United States?

- How has the religious composition of RA officers changed over time?
- What is the likely projected religious composition of RA officers over the next five years?
- What can we learn about the potential spiritual needs of individuals who report not having a religious affiliation ("Nones")?

We address these questions in the following chapters. Chapter Two provides an overview of the data and methodological approach used in the report. Chapter Three presents current and projected religious trends in the Army and provides detailed breakdowns by key denominational categories and religious families. Additionally, it compares religious trends for RA enlisted soldiers to trends for RA officers and chaplains. Chapter Three also includes an analysis of the individuals who report no religious affiliation, and the potential implications for the religious and spiritual needs of the future RA population. Chapter Four summarizes findings and discusses key takeaways from our analysis.

CHAPTER TWO

Methodology

This chapter provides a brief overview of the data and methods used in analyzing religious affiliation in the RA and in the U.S. population.

Data

Monthly administrative data on enlisted RA personnel were obtained from the Total Army Personnel Database for Active Enlisted Soldiers (TAPDB-AE). We also used monthly administrative data on RA chaplains and RA officers from the Total Army Personnel Database for Active Officers (TAPDB-AO). We compiled variables on all RA enlisted personnel from fiscal year (FY) 2001 to FY 2019, including information on soldiers' initial enlistment year, date of birth, permanent state of residence at time of enlistment, and religious affiliation (given by faith and belief codes per U.S. Department of Defense Manual [DODM] 7730.54, 2019). Using permanent state of residence (at time of enlistment), we can construct the geographic distribution of RA enlisted soldiers in each year in our sample. We also compiled information on the religious affiliation of all chaplains and officers from FY 2001 to FY 2019.

In most of our analyses, we remove incomplete observations from the TAPDB data; that is, we remove records for soldiers who are missing either geographic or religious affiliation information (in most cases, if one variable is missing, then both are missing). Because there is no way to know how missing values would affect the religious composition of the RA, we believe it is valid to simply exclude these cases.

To examine religious affiliation in the U.S. population, we use data from the GSS. The GSS is a project of the independent research organization the National Opinion Research Center (NORC), at the University of Chicago, with principal funding from the National Science Foundation (Smith et al., 2018). The data are available on a biyearly basis and use a full-probability sample design to produce a high-quality, representative sample of the adult population of the United States. We chose to use GSS data over other possible data sources because of its availability over time. We use region-level religious affiliation data, variables on religiosity (e.g., belief in God, spirituality, etc.), and demographic characteristics (i.e., age and gender) to analyze national religious trends.

Methodological Approach

We begin by examining the religious composition of enlisted RA soldiers. While the recruit population will change most dramatically in response to changing religious trends nationwide, we perform our analysis on the total enlisted RA population for two reasons. First, the total number of Army recruits per year is quite variable, while the total enlisted RA population is more stable over time. This is shown in Figure A.1, in the appendix. Because we cannot predict how many recruits there will be in future years, and existing variability increases the potential for error in our predictions, using the total population is a more plausible choice for predicting future changes in religious groups. Second, and more importantly, using the total population is more meaningful for DACH's purposes; if the religious composition of the Army changes because of the recruits in one year, those changes will persist as long as these soldiers remain in the Army. As such, understanding how the total enlisted RA population might change is critical for future planning.

Next, we compare that composition to the composition of the U.S. population. While the TAPDB-AE data contain 192 possible religious denominations, we classify these into major religious categories (Protestant, Catholic, Jewish, Islam, Orthodox Christian, Buddhism, Hindu, Eastern Religions, other religions, and "None") based on the religious groupings used by the GSS, and we compare the proportion of each across both populations. To make the two samples more comparable, we weight the religious composition in the GSS using the geographic, gender, and age distributions of enlisted soldiers. A more detailed breakdown of each variable, as well as a comparison of the two datasets, is available in the appendix of this report. Because the GSS is a representative sample of the country, the two populations (i.e., those captured in the TAPDB-AE and the weighted GSS) would look similar if the RA were generally representative of the U.S. population. If, however, certain populations and religious groups enlist and remain in the Army at different rates than others, this comparison highlights these differences.

We further break down the broad religious categories by denominational families in order to provide a more detailed analysis of trends in religious composition among enlisted soldiers. There is a considerable amount of diversity within the broad religious categories, especially within soldiers who identify as Protestants. We organize religious denominations into thematic groups, or families, that have similar traditions, practices, and historical roots. Specifically, we organize the 192 religions in the TAPDB data into 26 religious families based on the categorization developed by the Association of Religion Data Archives (ARDA). Families are classified by tracing the lineage of all major religions and grouping together those with similar historical origins and traditions into family trees.[1] The families identified by the ARDA also represent the most common religious denominations in the United States, and the categories that their members would likely use to identify themselves (e.g., a member of the Southern Baptist Conference would likely consider himself or herself a Baptist rather than a Protestant more generally). For reference, major ARDA families and broad religious categories from the GSS are shown in Table 2.1; only those that are represented in the TAPDB data are shown. See the appendix

---

[1] For more detailed descriptions of each family, see ARDA, undated. The families themselves were created by tracing detailed historical lineages of each religion using multiple sources. These sources include Reid et al., 1990; Melton, 2003; Mead, Hill, and Atwood, 2005; and Wiederaenders, 1998.

Table 2.1
Major Religious Groups and Corresponding Religious Families

Religious Group (GSS)	Religious Family (ARDA)
Protestant	Adventist, Anglican, Baptist, Christian Science, Congregational, European Free Church, Holiness, Independent Fundamentalist, Latter Day Saints, Liberal, Lutheran, Methodist, Other Protestant, Pentecostal, Reformed/Presbyterian, Protestant—No Denomination, Restoration, Spiritualist
Catholic	Catholic (Western Liturgical)
Orthodox Christian	Eastern Liturgical
Muslim/Islam	Islam
Jewish	Jewish
Native American	Native American
Buddhist	Other
Eastern	Other
Hindu	Other
Other	Other
None	None

SOURCES: ARDA, undated; GSS, undated; and TAPDB.

NOTE: This table depicts the religious groups (as defined by the GSS) and religious families that are represented in the TAPDB data. Some families, namely "Protestant—No Denomination" and "Other," did not fit into any of the ARDA's existing religious families, and were added to better fit the TAPDB data. It is also worth noting that the "Catholic (Western Liturgical)" family is referred to as "Catholic" throughout the text for simplicity.

for a much more detailed breakdown of the religious groups that make up each religious family, as well as the religious groups from the GSS.[2] We also compare the religious composition of enlisted soldiers to that of chaplains, using both aggregate categories and denominational families.

---

[2] Because there are 192 possible religious groups that a soldier can choose from, the table that illustrates the grouping of the broader categories and families is very long. As such, we include it for reference in the appendix.

One important distinction that is noticeably missing from our analysis is an identification of evangelical and Mainline Protestants. While it is particularly common to distinguish between these types of Protestantism (e.g., Pew Research Center, 2015), we were unable to make these distinctions using the TAPDB data for a few key reasons. Across datasets, the term "evangelical" is included in the names of some denominations, but many evangelical groups do not use this terminology explicitly. Therefore, forming these groups would require us, as researchers, to decide which groups count as evangelical and Mainline. On a related note, it is not clear whether there is one agreed-on categorization for evangelical and Mainline Protestants. For example, in the GSS, many researchers use a "RELTRAD" (religious tradition) coding scheme to separate Protestants into Mainline, evangelical, and Black Protestant traditions (Steensland et al., 2000). However, others have identified potential inconsistencies with this coding scheme and researchers' attempts to re-create the coding in statistical software (e.g., Stetzer and Burge, 2016). Within the Army data, "evangelical" is an option that soldiers can select to define their religion, but this affirmation results in a much lower and implausible percentage of evangelicals in the Army when compared with other data like those from GSS that are coded through RELTRAD.

While we could apply RELTRAD to the TAPDB, a significant obstacle for doing this is that "nondenominational" Protestant may mean different things in the Army data compared with other religious data sources. While nondenominational Protestants are typically grouped with evangelical Protestants (e.g., Steensland et al., 2000), there is reason to believe that many nondenominational Protestants in the Army data are not evangelical. Compared with the GSS, the nondenominational category is significantly larger in the TAPDB. As Figure 2.1 shows, while the percentage of evangelicals in the U.S. population has declined modestly in recent years, nondenominational Protestants have increased dramatically in the Army. This suggests that "nondenominational" could mean something different in the Army data than it does in the GSS.

Supporting this statistically based inference, discussions with RAND Arroyo Center Fellows indicated that many soldiers who iden-

Figure 2.1
Evangelical and Mainline Protestant Denominations in the Regular Enlisted Army and the U.S. Population

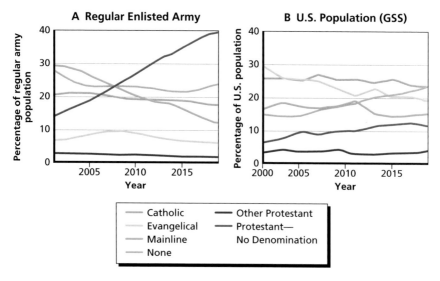

SOURCES: TAPDB-AE and GSS, undated; Steensland et al., 2000; and author's calculations.

NOTE: The figure shows Catholic, None, and Protestant populations in the RA and the U.S. population. Protestants are broken down by evangelical, Mainline, Other, and No Denomination, using Steensland et al.'s RELTRAD variable (for simplicity, Black Protestants are included in the "Evangelical" category). Although nondenominational Protestants are typically placed in the Evangelical category, the figure shows them separately to illustrate the discrepancies between the groups in the two data sources.

tify as nondenominational do not wish to specify a denominational preference during their service in the Army, possibly because they do not necessarily want to interact with DACH. Thus, including them in an evangelical category may greatly overestimate the true number of evangelicals in the RA population, while leaving them out may underestimate their true numbers. Given the potential inconsistencies for the coding of the evangelical category across datasets, we did not further analyze evangelical Protestants in this report.

Next, we project religious affiliation among enlisted RA soldiers for the largest religious groups. Projections are made based on three potential future scenarios. In Scenario 1, we assume that there are no changes in future recruitment patterns, and that the current geographic distribution of soldiers is constant. We regress the proportion of each religious group in the total enlisted RA population on the year and use the resulting model to predict values for FY 2020–2024. Because the change in a religious group from one year to the next is not perfectly linear, we use a second-order polynomial regression model to better capture the curvilinear trend. Because the data do not exhibit any seasonal or cyclical patterns, this simple regression model was preferable to a more complex forecasting method.

Scenario 2 assumes that the Army shifts its geographic recruitment patterns. For reference, U.S. states are mapped by geographic region in Figure 2.2; these regional designations are used throughout the report (U.S. Census Bureau, 2010). Based on the Army's interest in increasing recruitment from cities that are currently underrepresented in the Army population, many of which are coastal (e.g., Miles, 2019;

Figure 2.2
Aggregation of U.S. States into Regions

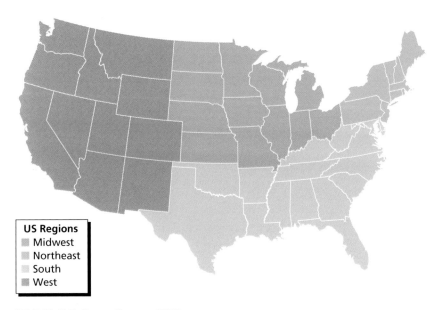

US Regions
Midwest
Northeast
South
West

SOURCE: U.S. Census Bureau, 2010.

Philipps, 2019), we hypothetically show how the religious composition would change if the Army were to increase the number of enlisted soldiers it recruits from the West and the Northeast. We increase the total number of RA enlisted soldiers from each region by 5 percent each and decrease total enlisted soldiers from the South and Midwest by the same amount. In this scenario, we assume that the Army's future soldiers are sampled from populations that mirror current enlisted soldiers, and that the only change is in the proportion of soldiers from each region. To make the projection, we take the current religious composition of all enlisted soldiers in the Army and recompute it using regional weights that match the new geographic scenario. We then perform the same second-order polynomial regression from the first scenario to obtain predicted values for FY 2020–2024.

Lastly, Scenario 3 considers what the religious composition of the Army would look like if (a) geographic recruitment patterns shifted by the amount in Scenario 2, and (b) shifting these recruitment patterns caused the religious composition of the Army to look more like the religious composition of the U.S. population overall. We first weight both the TAPDB-AE and GSS data regionally to match the new geographic distribution of soldiers. Since the RA population is significantly more male than the population captured in the GSS (85 percent in TAPDB-AE compared with 45 percent in the GSS), we also weight the GSS data by gender to better match the underlying population from which the RA is recruited. The RA is also younger than the GSS population, and we only include respondents under the age of 55 from the GSS in the calculation.[3] Then we take the average of the proportion in each religious group in each dataset. An illustration of these average values can be found in the appendix. We use these new average proportions to make projections for FY 2020–2024, using the same method as above. We expect the mean value to be the upper bound for the true outcome; in reality, the new religious composition might fall somewhere between Scenarios 2 and 3 in response to the hypothetical change in recruiting patterns.

---

[3] Because response rates are somewhat lower for individuals ages 18 to 24 in the GSS, we opted not to weight the data by age to avoid severely limiting the sample size.

It is important to note that these projections reweight the religious affiliations of *all* soldiers, not just new recruits. They should therefore not be considered exact predictions of how religious affiliation will evolve in the immediate future, as this will depend on religious affiliation not only among new recruits, but also among current soldiers. Rather, the projections should be seen as a way to illustrate how the religious makeup of the Army might change in response to shifting recruitment efforts and the corresponding change in the geographic makeup of the Army that they might induce.

Additionally, we use officer data (TAPDB-AO) not only to identify chaplains, but also to analyze the religious composition of RA officers, to whom chaplains also provide religious services. We project the religious composition among RA officers, assuming there are no changes in recruitment patterns (Scenario 1).

Finally, we use the GSS data to investigate the potential spiritual needs of individuals who do not affiliate with a specific religion (namely, members of the "None" category). The majority of soldiers in this category report having "no religious preference," although a very small percentage (less than 4 percent) identify as atheist or agnostic. To perform this analysis, we construct our own "spirituality" variable from the GSS data, using a combination of variables on participation in religious activities, belief in God, and whether the respondent considers himself or herself to be a "spiritual person." Variables were chosen primarily based on data availability: most other related variables are available inconsistently or cannot be traced over time. Additionally, these variables tend to be commonly used in related research on the religiosity of "Nones" (e.g., Lim, MacGregor, and Putnam, 2010; Hout and Fischer, 2002). A detailed breakdown of this variable can be found in the appendix; complete reporting of all variables is only available in the GSS starting in 2008, and our analysis begins in that year.[4]

The "spirituality" variable takes on a value of one if, at minimum, a respondent in the "None" category reports believing in a higher power of some kind, that he or she is "slightly spiritual," or that he or she partici-

---

[4]   These variables were introduced into the GSS in 2006 but were not answered by all respondents until 2008.

pates in religious activities more often than "never." Otherwise, the variable takes on a value of zero. Some people who identify as "None" may actually be moderately or very spiritual; to better capture the diversity within this category, we also create a "moderately spiritual" variable. This variable takes a one if a person reports believing in a God more often than "sometimes" or reports that he or she is at least "moderately" spiritual, or if he or she participates in religious activities at least multiple times a year.

This analysis can shed light on the potential share of soldiers in the "None" category who may benefit from having access to religious services. However, we caution that this analysis is based on GSS data from the U.S. population, and that the enlisted RA soldier population may be different from the nation as a whole in this respect.

CHAPTER THREE

Findings

We first provide an overview of the religious affiliation of enlisted RA soldiers, and then compare the religious affiliation of enlisted soldiers with the religious affiliation in the United States as a whole, as well as with the religious affiliation of Army chaplains. We then provide projections of religious affiliation of enlisted RA soldiers, following the three scenarios described in Chapter Two. Next, we analyze trends in the religious composition of RA officers. Finally, we examine in more detail the preferences of individuals who report not being affiliated with a religion.

Before showing the results of our analysis, it is important to note that a small proportion of observations from the TAPDB-AE are missing information about religious affiliation and the key geographic variable we use: state of permanent residence at the time of enlistment. As Figure 3.1 shows, around 2 percent of observations are missing geographic information, and 7 percent of observations are missing religious affiliation information.[1] As there is no way to know how the missing information would change our analysis if it were available, we generally exclude these observations from our investigation (with the exception of a few initial figures in which missing values are displayed in order to illustrate how they affect overall trends).

---

[1]   There are 7,897,260 observations in the TAPDB-AE dataset, and many are repeat observations of the same soldiers over time. This percentage is based on the number of observations with missing data.

Figure 3.1
Percentage of Observations Missing Religious Affiliation or State of Permanent Residence at the Time of Enlistment by Year

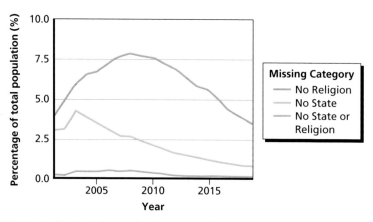

SOURCE: Author's calculations using TAPDB-AE data.

NOTE: The graph depicts the percentage of observations missing information on religious affiliation, state of permanent residence at the time of enlistment, or both, in the TAPDB-AE data by year.

Overview: The Religious Composition of Enlisted Regular Army Soldiers

Figure 3.2 shows the religious composition of enlisted RA soldiers. Panel A presents religious groups by total numbers and shows that the total number of enlisted RA soldiers has fluctuated considerably over time. To get a more standardized measure of the religious composition of the RA, which is not heavily influenced by fluctuations in end strength, Panel B shows religious composition as a proportion of the total enlisted RA soldier population.

As discussed above, the administrative records for the religious affiliation variable are missing for many soldiers, which is illustrated using the dotted gray "Missing" line. The share of soldiers for whom information on religious affiliation is missing or not available (NA) increases in the mid-2000s and declines afterward. Note that "NA" indicates that there is no information on religious affiliation available for the soldier. This is distinct from the "None" category. For the "None" category, informa-

Figure 3.2
Religious Composition Among Enlisted RA Soldiers, FY 2001–2019

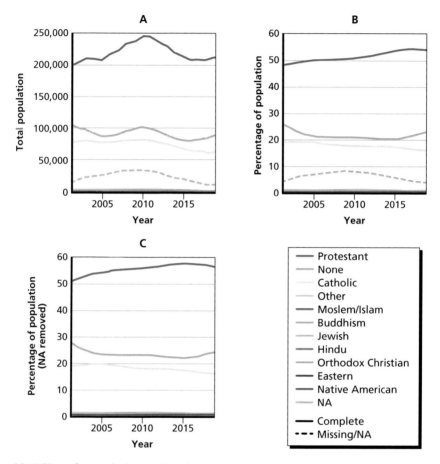

SOURCE: Author's calculations based on TAPDB data.
NOTE: Panel A shows the number of enlisted RA soldiers by religious affiliation, while Panel B shows the share of enlisted RA soldiers by religious affiliation. NA values are shown using a gray dotted line for emphasis. Panel C shows the same shares, with observations for which information on religious affiliation or state of permanent residence at the time of enlistment is missing removed (note the lack of an "NA" line).

tion is available about religious affiliation; it comprises individuals who identify as atheists (3 percent of the "None" group) and agnostics (0.2 percent), and those who report having "no religion" (the largest group of the three, comprising 96 percent of the "None" category).

Panel C depicts the religious groups as a proportion of the population for whom we have information on religious affiliation (that is, with all NA values removed) and for whom we have information on state of permanent residence at the time of enlistment. Panel C highlights the impact of missing values on the percentages: Although the general religious affiliation patterns are the same, the curves representing the three largest religious groups (Protestants, "Nones," and Catholics) shift upward when NA values are dropped. Because we cannot know for sure how these missing values would change the distribution of religious affiliation (if at all), we use the proportions from Panel C for most calculations.

As shown in Panel C, the majority of enlisted RA soldiers identify as Protestant. "Nones" and Catholics are the second- and third-largest groups, making up around 24 and 16 percent of the enlisted RA population, respectively, in FY 2019. The share of Protestants has increased in recent years, while the share of Catholics has declined. All other religious groups make up approximately 1 percent or less of the enlisted soldier population.

Figure 3.3 shows the same data from Panel C, but only for the small religious groups. Aside from Protestants, Catholics, and "Nones," all other religious groups make up approximately 1 percent or less of the enlisted RA population. Although some groups, such as Buddhists and Muslims, have experienced modest increases in recent years, most have maintained a stable proportion of the Army population.

Next, we consider how religious affiliation varies by geographic region of origin. Panel A of Figure 3.4 illustrates the state of permanent residence (at time of enlistment)[2] of RA enlisted soldiers over the FY 2001–2019 period. Unsurprisingly, states with the highest populations account for a large percentage of enlisted RA soldiers. More soldiers are from Texas (10.1 percent) and California (9.8 percent), which account collectively for around 20 percent of the population, than from any other state (Table 3.1). The gap between Texas and California and the

---

[2]   Note that state of permanent residence (at time of enlistment) is the state in which a soldier was residing when he or she was enlisted into the RA. This is not the state where a soldier is stationed.

Figure 3.3
RA Religious Composition: Small Religions

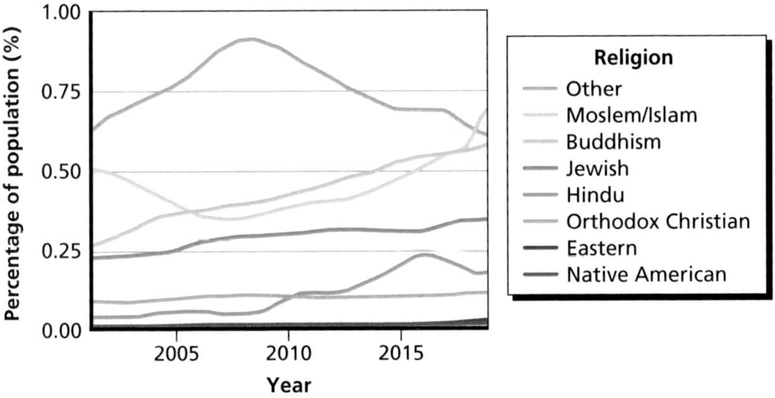

SOURCE: TAPDB-AE and author's own calculations.
NOTE: The graph shows the percentage of the enlisted RA population in each small religious group. Each group makes up 1 percent or less of the RA population.

next-highest state (Florida) is nearly 40,000 soldiers over the entire time period. The religious preferences of soldiers from these highly represented states are likely an important driver of the religious composition of the total enlisted population.

Panel B of Figure 3.4 illustrates the same number of soldiers, divided by the 2018 population for each state; the number of soldiers is highest on a per-capita basis from Texas, South Carolina, and Georgia. Figure 3.5 illustrates the region of permanent residence (at the time of enlistment) among enlisted RA soldiers over time. Almost 50 percent of all enlisted RA soldiers are from southern states, while the West, Midwest, and Northeast make up a comparatively smaller proportion of the population.

Figure 3.6 shows the religious composition of the enlisted RA by the region from which each soldier was recruited. In every region, Protestant is the largest category, followed by "None" and Catholic. Protestants make up the highest proportion (over 60 percent) of enlisted RA soldiers from the South, followed by approximately 55 percent in the Midwest, 45 percent in the West, and 40 percent in the Northeast.

Figure 3.4
Total and Per-Capita Numbers of Enlisted RA Soldiers by State,
FY 2001–2019

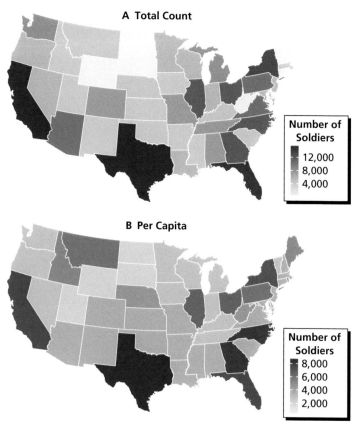

SOURCE: Author's calculations from TAPDB-AE and U.S. Census Bureau, 2018, data.

NOTE: Panel A maps the total number of soldiers who list each state as their state of permanent residence (at time of enlistment). Panel B maps the same values divided by the 2018 population for each state to produce per capita estimates. To simplify the map, Alaska and Hawaii are not pictured (but are included in subsequent analyses as states in the Western region of the United States). Maps show locations of all soldiers with geographic information (soldiers missing religious affiliation data are not excluded here).

Table 3.1
Number of Enlisted RA Soldiers by State of Permanent Residence at Time of Enlistment, Top Ten States, FY 2001–2019

State	Total Enlisted Soldiers	Percentage of RA Soldiers
Texas	157,393	10.16
California	152,237	9.83
Florida	113,605	7.34
New York	71,722	4.63
Georgia	65,866	4.26
North Carolina	61,218	3.95
Ohio	52,397	3.38
Virginia	50,117	3.24
Illinois	49,328	3.19
Pennsylvania	47,487	3.07

SOURCE: Author's calculations from TAPDB-AE data.

NOTE: The table shows the total number of enlisted soldiers from each state, added across all years (2001–2019), and the percentage of the total RA population that each state makes up.

The "None" group makes up approximately 30 percent of enlisted RA soldiers from the Northeast, West, and Midwest, and approximately 20 percent of soldiers from the South. The largest Catholic populations are in the Northeast (between 20 and 30 percent) and West (just over 20 percent). Catholics make up a smaller proportion of enlisted RA soldiers from the South and Midwest, at 10–15 percent. The overall religious composition among enlisted RA soldiers most closely resembles the religious makeup of soldiers from the South, which is consistent with the fact that nearly half of all soldiers are recruited from southern states.

Figure 3.5
RA Enlisted Soldiers by Region of Permanent Residence at
Time of Enlistment, FY 2001–2019

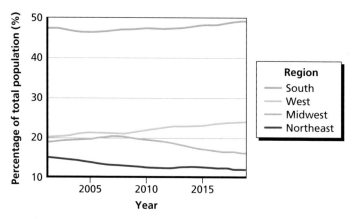

SOURCE: Author's calculations using TAPDB-AE data.

NOTE: Percentage of RA enlisted soldiers who report a state in each region as their state of permanent residence at the time of enlistment. For reference, this graph does not exclude soldiers who do not report religious affiliation information.

Comparison with the United States Population

Figure 3.7 compares the religious composition of enlisted RA soldiers with that of the U.S. population using GSS data. We show the composition of both the full TAPDB-AE dataset, and TAPDB-AE data with observations that are missing religious affiliation or state of permanent residence at the time of enlistment removed. Slightly over 20 percent of the U.S. population reports a Catholic religious affiliation, compared with a little over 15 percent among enlisted RA soldiers. In contrast, after removing the TAPDB-AE records for which religious affiliation or state of permanent residence at the time of enlistment are NA, the share of enlisted RA soldiers reporting a Protestant religious affiliation is nearly 60 percent, compared with less than 50 percent for the overall U.S. population. The share of "Nones" in the TAPDB-AE (a little over 20 percent) is similar to the share of individuals reporting "None" in the U.S. population.

Figure 3.6
Religious Composition of RA Enlisted Soldiers by Region of Permanent Residence at Time of Enlistment, FY 2001–2019

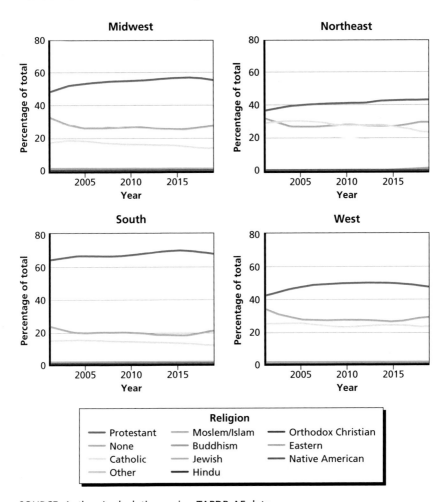

SOURCE: Authors' calculations using TAPDB-AE data.

NOTE: Each panel shows the percentage of soldiers in each religious category over time, broken down by region of permanent residence. NA values are removed.

Figure 3.7
Comparing the Religious Composition Among Enlisted RA Soldiers and the U.S. Population, 2018

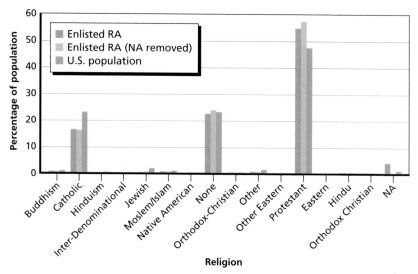

SOURCE: Author's calculations using data from TAPDB-AE and GSS data, undated.
NOTE: Proportions of respondents in each religious category among enlisted RA soldiers and the overall U.S. population. Data are from 2018 (the most recent date for GSS data). For enlisted soldiers, proportions are shown with and without observations that are missing religious affiliation and/or state of permanent residence at the time of enlistment ("NA").

Figure 3.8 compares religious affiliation among enlisted RA soldiers and the overall U.S. population over time. In this case, we only include observations on enlisted RA soldiers for which religious affiliation and state of permanent residence at the time of enlistment are available in the TAPDB-AE. The largest difference between these two populations is in the Protestant category: While the percentage of Protestants in the U.S. has been steadily declining since 2000, the share of Protestants in the enlisted RA has increased over time. The share of those reporting "None" in the overall U.S. population has risen from 15 percent in 2000 to 25 percent by 2018, while the share of "Nones" in the enlisted RA has fallen slightly, from nearly 30 percent to about 25 percent, during the same time period. The shares of Catholics in both datasets are trending slightly downward, with the share of Catho-

Figure 3.8
Comparing Religious Affiliation Among Enlisted RA Soldiers and the
Overall U.S. Population over Time

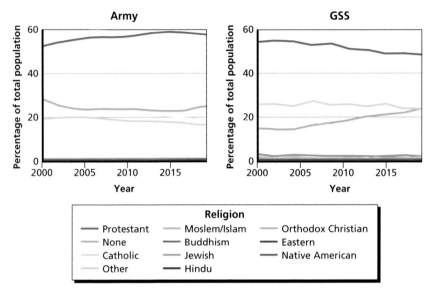

SOURCE: Author's calculations using data from TAPDB-AE and GSS, undated.
NOTE: Percentage of respondents in each religious category over time. The left panel
presents this information for enlisted RA soldiers, while the right panel presents this
information for the overall U.S. population. Observations missing religious affiliation
and/or state of permanent residence at the time of enlistment are excluded.

lics in the U.S. population about 5 percentage points higher than the
share in the enlisted RA.

It is, however, slightly misleading to compare the enlisted RA to
the entire United States, as enlisted soldiers are drawn from a younger
and more regionally concentrated subset of the population. Therefore,
we produce one final figure comparing the two datasets, in which the
GSS data are weighted by the age, gender, and regional composition
found in the TAPDB-AE data. For example, by applying the weighting, younger individuals, men, and those from the South, who more
closely resemble the population represented by the enlisted RA, are
more heavily weighted than older respondents from the Northeast (or a
similar group that is less represented in the enlisted RA).

Figure 3.9 shows the religious composition from the TAPDB-AE (Panel A) and the weighted GSS (Panel B). Individuals in this weighted version of the GSS tend to be less Protestant, and less Catholic, than the overall U.S. population; they are more likely to be in the "None" category. In this case, the Protestant groups in the enlisted RA and the U.S. population are even more divergent over time, illustrating that enlisted RA soldiers look considerably different from the general recruiting-age population. This may be the case for many reasons. For example, there may be a selection effect, as people with certain identities join and remain in the military at different rates than others. This may also be the result of Army recruitment efforts being concentrated in certain regions with particular characteristics. While we address these scenarios in more depth later in the report, our data do not provide enough information to explain the causes of these patterns.

Figure 3.9
Comparing Religious Affiliation Among Enlisted RA Soldiers and the Overall U.S. Population (Weighted by Age, Gender, and Region) over Time

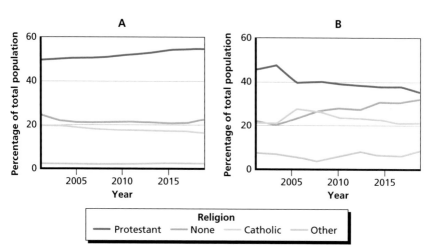

SOURCES: Author's calculations using data from TAPDB-AE and GSS, undated.
NOTE: The figure compares the religious composition of the enlisted RA (Panel A) with the religious composition of the GSS (Panel B). The GSS data have been weighted by region, gender, and age to match the relative composition of the enlisted RA data. The smallest religious groups (<1 percent of each population) are aggregated into the "other" category to improve the readability of the graph. Observations missing religious affiliation and/or state of permanent residence at the time of enlistment are excluded.

A Closer Look: Breaking It Down by Detailed Denominational Families

Next, we break down the religious composition of the enlisted RA by more detailed religious families, as described in Chapter Two. Figure 3.10 depicts the total number of enlisted RA soldiers in each major religious family in FY 2018. The largest families represented by soldiers are Protestant (no denomination), "None," Catholic, and Baptist. Methodist, Restoration, Pentecostal, Lutheran, Holiness, Latter Day Saints, and "Other" are modestly represented in the enlisted RA population, and all other groups make up a comparatively small number of soldiers.

Figure 3.10
Number of Enlisted RA Soldiers by Religious Family, FY 2018

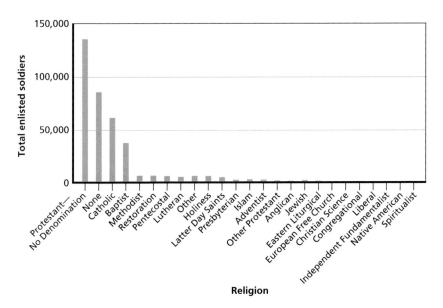

SOURCE: Author's calculations using data and religious family classification from TAPDB-AE data and religious family classification from ARDA, undated.
NOTE: Total number of enlisted RA soldiers in each religious family in FY 2018. Observations missing religious affiliation and/or state of permanent residence at the time of enlistment are excluded.

Figure 3.11 shows the proportion of the RA population represented by each religious family over time. To improve readability, the largest religious families are graphed in the left panel, while those that make up less than 5 percent of the population are presented in the right

Figure 3.11
Proportion of Enlisted RA Soldiers by Religious Family, FY 2001–2019

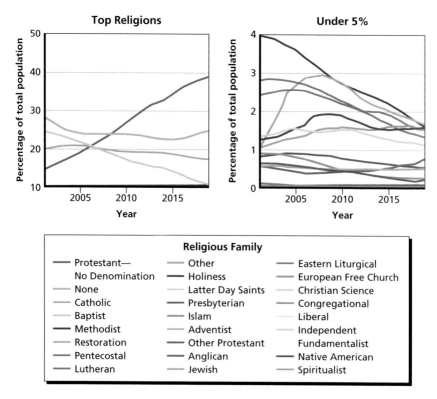

SOURCE: Author's calculations using TAPDB-AE and religious family classification from ARDA, undated.

NOTE: Share of enlisted RA soldiers in each religious family over time. Because graphing all religious families at once creates a somewhat visually cluttered graph, we display the religions that account for the largest percentage of the population in the left panel, and the remaining religions (which make up less than 5 percent of the population) in the right panel. Colors in the legend are ordered by the ranking of each religion in the data using the percentage of the population when all years are pooled. Observations missing religious affiliation and/or state of permanent residence at the time of enlistment are excluded.

panel. In this figure, Protestant (no denomination), "None," Catholic, and Baptist are the largest religious families over time. The most striking feature of the left panel is the sharp increase in the share of soldiers who report that they are Protestants but do not identify with a denomination. A range of simple and more complex mechanisms may be driving this trend. For example, this could be the result of a change in the way that the administrative data are collected, prompting soldiers to opt for nonspecific religious designations in lieu of choosing from other denominational options. It could be that soldiers are equally religious as before but increasingly wish to opt out of participating in religious services and activities; choosing a nonspecific designation may enable them to do so more easily. It could signify an overall decline in religiosity. Alternatively, it could reflect an increase within the RA in conservative forms of evangelical Christianity that do not expressly affiliate with any historically established Protestant denominations. Further research is needed to make sense of what is driving this trend, and what it ultimately means for DACH.

Finally, Figure 3.12 displays trends in the proportion of soldiers in each religious family by region of permanent residence at the time of enlistment. While there are similar patterns across all regions, there are important regional distinctions. In all regions, Protestant (no denomination) is increasing. It has increased the most among soldiers from the South and coincides with the decline in Baptists in that region. By 2019, Protestant (no denomination) was the largest religious family in all regions except the Northeast, where "None" was the largest. "None" is the second-most-common in all three other regions, although it has only recently displaced Baptists as the second-highest group in the South. Baptists are the fourth-largest denomination among soldiers from all regions except the South, where they are the third largest; the share of enlisted RA soldiers reporting a Baptist religious affiliation is declining among soldiers from all four regions. The highest proportion of Catholics is among soldiers from the Northeast, followed by the West, Midwest, and South. The other large families make up approximately 5 percent or less of the population in each region, and most appear to be either declining or experiencing little growth over time.

Figure 3.12
Proportion of Enlisted RA Soldiers by Religious Family and Region of Permanent Residence at the Time of Enlistment

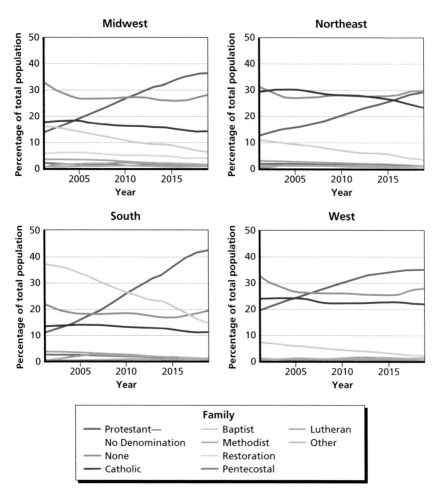

SOURCE: Author's calculations using TAPDB-AE data and religious family classification from ARDA, undated.

NOTE: Share of soldiers in each religious family over time. The panels organize this information by soldiers' region of permanent residence at the time of enlistment. Only the ten largest religious families are shown; all other religious families make up approximately 1 percent or less of the enlisted RA population. Observations missing religious affiliation and/or state of permanent residence at the time of enlistment are excluded.

Religious Affiliation of Regular Army Chaplains

Next, we compare the current religious composition of the enlisted RA with that of RA chaplains. Figure 3.13 illustrates this comparison using the broad religious categories. It is worth noting that although "NA" values for religion are removed (as in previous analyses), fewer than 1 percent of chaplains are missing religious information. RA chaplains are largely Protestant; in recent years, Protestant chaplains have made up approximately 80–90 percent of chaplains. Further, the proportion of Protestant chaplains is substantially greater than the proportion of Protestant soldiers (just under 60 percent in FY 2019). In contrast, the proportion of Catholic chaplains (about 6 percent) is lower than the proportion of Catholic soldiers by around 10 percentage points. All other religious groups make up a small proportion of both the RA's enlisted soldiers and its chaplains.

Next, we consider what this means for enlisted soldiers' access to chaplains who share the same religious affiliation. Figure 3.14 illus-

Figure 3.13
Comparison of the Religious Composition of RA Enlisted Soldiers and Chaplains, FY 2001–2019

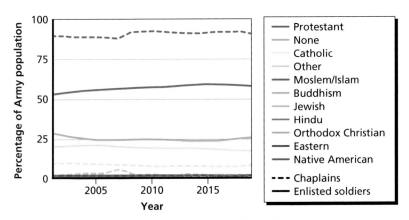

SOURCE: Author's calculations using TAPDB-AE and TAPDB-AO data.
NOTE: Proportion of RA enlisted soldiers in each major religious category (solid lines), compared with the proportion of RA chaplains in each major religious category (dashed lines). Observations missing religious affiliation and/or state of permanent residence at the time of enlistment are excluded from the enlisted soldier data.

trates the number of RA chaplains in each religious category per 1,000 enlisted RA soldiers in the corresponding category. While there are comparatively many chaplains per soldier for a number of the smaller religious groups, the rate is noticeably lower for the largest religious groups, Protestants and Catholics. For every 1,000 soldiers in one of these categories, there are, on average, six Protestant chaplains and one Catholic chaplain. This further highlights the discrepancy between the number of Catholics in the enlisted RA and in DACH. This, however, does not necessarily indicate that Catholic chaplains are being under-recruited or are reluctant to join DACH. According to the Georgetown University Center for Applied Research in the Apostolate, there are 0.5 Catholic priests for every 1,000 Catholics in the United States (i.e., one

Figure 3.14
Regular Chaplains per Thousand Soldiers by Religious Category

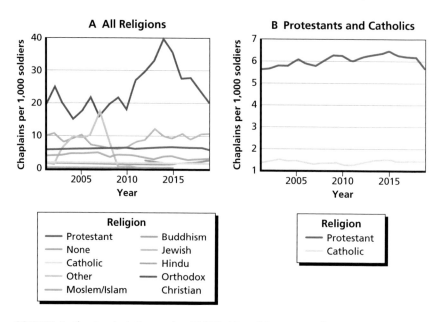

SOURCE: Author's calculations using TAPDB-AE and TAPDB-AO data.
NOTE: Number of RA chaplains in each religious category for every 1,000 enlisted RA soldiers in that category. The left panel shows this calculation for all religious categories, and the right panel shows only Protestants and Catholics, the two largest categories. Observations missing religious affiliation and/or state of permanent residence at the time of enlistment are excluded from the enlisted soldier data.

priest per 2,000 Catholics) (Center for Applied Research in the Apostolate, undated). This would indicate that Catholic priests are present in DACH at a rate that is fully twice the base rate of Catholic priests in the relevant U.S. population.

Lastly, we consider how chaplains' denominational families compare with the distribution of families across enlisted RA soldiers. Figure 3.15 illustrates the religious family composition of chaplains. As in

Figure 3.15
RA Chaplains by Religious Family, FY 2001–2019

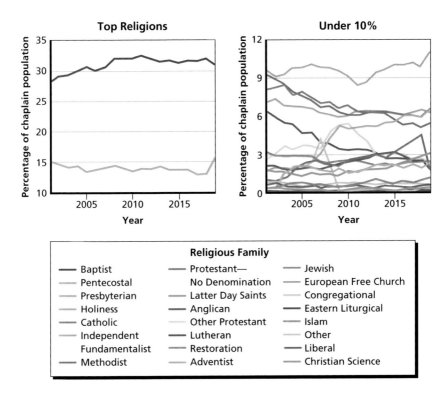

SOURCE: Author's calculations using TAPDB-AO data and the ARDA religious family classifications from ARDA, undated.
NOTE: Share of RA chaplains in each religious family over time. To improve readability, the left panel presents the top two religious families, and the right panel presents all religious families that make up 10 percent or less of the RA chaplain population. Note that the order of the colors is based on the ranking of religious families in the chaplain population. Observations that are missing religious informa-

Figure 3.11, the left panel shows the two largest denominational families, while the right panel shows the smaller families. The largest group of chaplains is Baptists, at over 30 percent of the chaplain population. The next largest is Pentecostals at just over 15 percent, Presbyterians at around 10 percent, and Catholic, Independent Fundamentalist, Holiness, and Methodist at approximately 5–6 percent of the population.

Figure 3.16 directly compares the religious family composition of the chaplains with that of enlisted soldiers for the five largest religious families (Protestant—no denomination, Catholic, Baptist, Methodist, and Restoration). From this figure, we can see that the makeup of the chaplains is substantially different from that of enlisted RA soldiers. One of the largest discrepancies is that, while Baptists are the largest religious family among chaplains, they only account for around 10 percent of the enlisted soldier population. Chaplains are also significantly more likely to identify as Methodist than enlisted RA soldiers, while the enlisted RA has a higher proportion of Catholics than

Figure 3.16
Comparison of RA Chaplains and Enlisted Soldiers by Religious Family

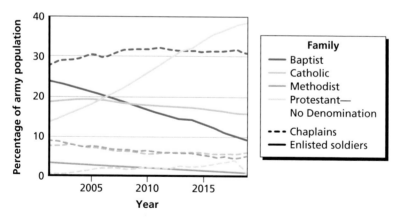

SOURCE: Author's calculations using TAPDB-AE and TAPDB-AO data and the ARDA religious family classifications from ARDA, undated.

NOTE: Share of RA chaplains in each religious family over time, compared with the share of enlisted RA soldiers. To improve readability, only the top five families (based on the RA enlisted soldier data) are shown. Observations missing religious affiliation and/or state of permanent residence at the time of enlistment are excluded from the enlisted soldier data.

DACH does. Another key difference is that the rise of nondenominational Protestants among enlisted soldiers is not reflected by the changing composition of the chaplains. While nearly 40 percent of enlisted soldiers do not identify with a particular denomination, less than 5 percent of chaplains are nondenominational. However, without more research into the characteristics of the nondenominational soldiers, it is hard to know whether this indicates that this group's needs are not being met; it may be that chaplains with training in a specific denomination can still meet the religious needs of these soldiers.

Projections by Recruiting Scenarios

Next, we use the data to forecast the religious composition of the enlisted RA under a baseline scenario (Scenario 1) and under two different recruitment scenarios (Scenarios 2 and 3). Recall that, as discussed in Chapter Two, Scenarios 2 and 3 reweight the religious affiliations of *all* enlisted soldiers, not just new recruits. Our projections should therefore be considered illustrative of how the religious makeup of the RA might change in response to shifting recruitment efforts, rather than exact predictions for how the religious composition will change by 2024; the latter will depend largely on religious affiliation among *current* soldiers. Because the following analysis uses shifting regional recruitment patterns to make predictions, soldiers who do not report a state of permanent residence (at time of enlistment), those who resided outside of the contiguous United States at time of enlistment (with the exception of residents of Alaska and Hawaii), and those who do not report any religious affiliation are excluded from the projections. This accounts for approximately 9 percent of all observations[3] in the TAPDB-AE data.

It is important to note that we did not create projections for the smaller religious groups in the RA. While Protestants, Catholics, and

---

[3] There are 7,897,262 total observations in the TAPDB-AE dataset, and many are soldiers with repeat observations over time. This number reflects the percentage of missing observations, and not the percentage of unique soldiers.

"Nones" make up a large proportion of soldiers, all other religions consistently make up less than 1 percent of the RA population. Even in cases where the proportion of small religious groups has increased (e.g., Muslims), the gains have been relatively modest, and we do not anticipate that DACH will need to make significant changes to account for this. For a number of small religions, the number of current chaplains per soldier is already high relative to other religious groups.

Figure 3.17 presents the projections for Scenario 1. The dashed line represents the prediction for each religious group, which is our best estimate of how the proportion of each religion will change over time. While the dashed line is our best estimate for how religious composition might change, it is only an estimate. The gray shaded area shows the 95-percent prediction interval around the estimate; we expect that around 95 percent of future values will fall within our prediction intervals if future trends continue to follow the same trajectory as in previous years.

If there is no change in geographic recruitment patterns, we expect that the proportion of Protestants in the RA will experience a modest

Figure 3.17
Forecasting the Religious Composition of the Enlisted RA (Scenario 1)

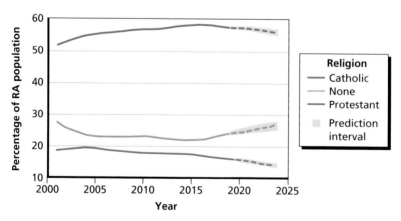

SOURCE: Author's calculations using TAPDB-AE data.
NOTE: The figure shows the current proportion of the three largest religious groups using solid lines, and the projected proportions using dashed lines. The gray boxes illustrate 95-percent prediction intervals.

decline of around 1 percentage point. The percentage of soldiers who report no religious affiliation ("Nones") will likely increase by around 3 percentage points, although the true increase could be between 0 and 5 percentage points. We project that Catholics will decline as a percentage of the RA population, by approximately 1 to 2 percentage points.

Although these percentage-point values seem small, the changes in the total RA population may be substantial. For every 100,000 soldiers, there are currently approximately 57,000 Protestants, 24,000 "Nones," and 16,000 Catholics. The projected changes would result in a decrease of around 1,000 Protestant soldiers, an increase of 3,000 soldiers who identify as "None," and a decrease of around 2,000 Catholic soldiers, for every 100,000 soldiers.[4]

As noted above, there are approximately six Protestant chaplains for every 1,000 Protestant soldiers, and one Catholic chaplain for every 1,000 Catholic soldiers. Thus, maintaining the same chaplain-soldier ratios given the projected changes would suggest that for every 100,000 enlisted soldiers, the number of Protestant chaplains could decrease by around six, while the number of Catholic chaplains could decrease by around two.[5] It is important to note that these values are entirely hypothetical and are intended to illustrate the magnitude of the projected changes.

Figure 3.18 graphs the results of Scenario 2, which considers how the religious composition of the RA might change if recruitment shifted toward more coastal cities that are currently underrepresented by incoming recruits (we proxy this change by shifting 10 percent of the enlisted RA population to the Northeast and West, and 10 percent away from the South and Midwest). This scenario uses the existing

---

[4]   In this analysis, we do not attempt to make projections for the total number of RA enlisted soldiers in each religious category. The end strength of the Army does not necessarily grow organically, but is subject to changes in recruiting efforts, exogenous geopolitical shocks, economic conditions, and other factors that we cannot account for.

[5]   This is calculated as follows: For every 1,000 Protestant soldiers, there are six Protestant chaplains, for a ratio of 0.006 chaplains to soldiers. Therefore, if the number of Protestant soldiers decreases by 1,000, the number of Protestant chaplains could decrease by 1,000*0.006 = 6 while maintaining the same ratio. Similar calculations are performed for Catholic chaplains.

Figure 3.18
Forecasting the Religious Composition of the Enlisted RA (Scenario 2)

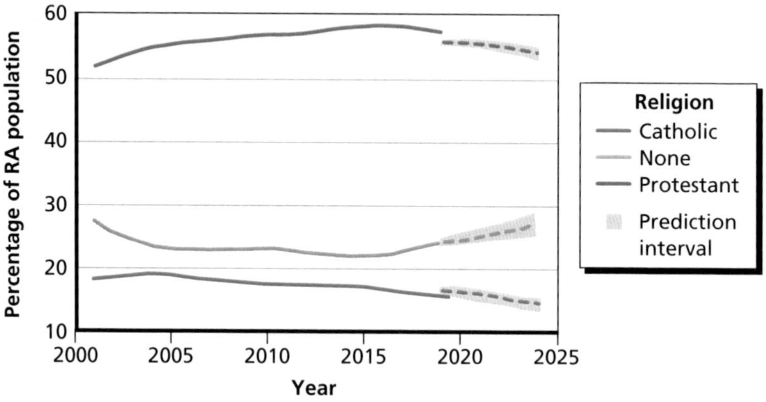

SOURCE: Author's calculations using TAPDB-AE data.
NOTE: The figure shows the current proportions of the three largest religious groups using solid lines, and the projected proportions using dashed lines. The predictions in this scenario are made by regionally reweighting the current values in the TAPDB-AE by the new recruiting scenario. The gray boxes illustrate 95-percent prediction intervals.

regional distribution of religious affiliation among enlisted RA soldiers to make projections about the future. Changes based on this scenario are fairly modest, with a decline in Protestants of approximately 3 percentage points, an increase in "Nones" of approximately 3.5 percentage points, and a slight decrease in Catholics of approximately 0.8 percentage points. Although these differences seem quite small when comparing percentage-point changes, they are much more substantial when we consider hypothetical changes in the total Army population. Compared with Scenario 1, for every 100,000 soldiers this would mean nearly 2,000 fewer Protestants, 1,000 additional soldiers in the "None" category, and 1,000 additional Catholics. To maintain the existing chaplain-soldier ratios, this scenario would require, for every 100,000 soldiers, 12 fewer Protestant chaplains than in Scenario 1 and one more Catholic chaplain than in Scenario 1.

Lastly, Figure 3.19 graphs Scenario 3, which is the most extreme of the three projections. This scenario considers how the religious composition among enlisted RA soldiers might change if shifting recruit-

Figure 3.19
Forecasting the Religious Composition of the Enlisted RA (Scenario 3)

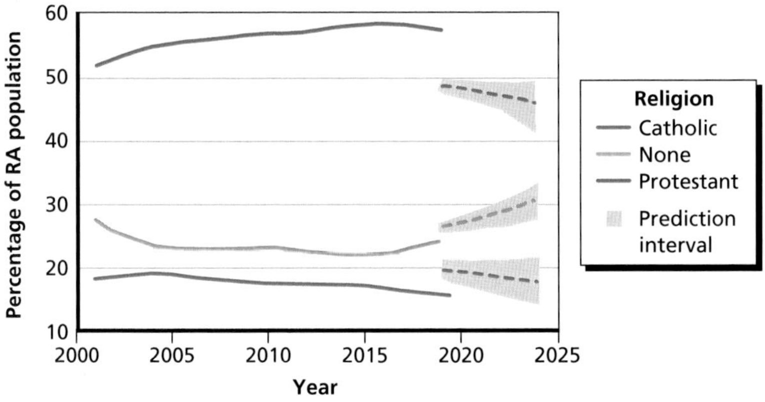

SOURCE: Author's calculations using TAPDB-AE data.
NOTE: The figure shows the current proportion of the three largest religious groups using solid lines, and the projected proportions using dashed lines. The predictions in this scenario are made by regionally reweighting the current values in the TAPDB-AE and GSS by the new recruiting scenario as well as the gender-distribution of the RA population (the reweighted values are shown in the appendix), and taking the mean between them. The gray boxes illustrate 95-percent prediction intervals.

ment patterns cause it to mirror trends in the religious composition of the U.S. population. This is accomplished by taking an average of the geographically weighted and gender-weighted TAPDB-AE and GSS data, as described in Chapter Two. As Figure 3.18 illustrates, this scenario would constitute a substantial shift from the current trajectory of major religious groups. This model predicts that the Protestant share of the enlisted RA would fall by approximately 12 percentage points, while soldiers indicating no religious affiliation ("Nones") would increase by 7 percentage points, and the Catholic share would increase by approximately 1 percentage point (although this latter value is decreasing over time). Compared with Scenario 1, for every 100,000 soldiers, this would mean a reduction in Protestants by 11,000, an increase in "Nones" by 5,000, and an increase in Catholics by 3,000. To maintain the existing chaplain-soldier ratios, this scenario would require, for every 100,000 soldiers, 66 fewer Protestant chaplains than in Scenario 1 and three more Catholic chaplains than in Scenario 1.

While it is extremely unlikely that the Army would experience these exact hypothetical changes, they illustrate just how much a small percentage-point change in geographic recruitment patterns could potentially change the religious composition of the military. The geography of Army recruiting is an important determinant of the future of religion among Army personnel and has the potential to substantially shift the religious and spiritual needs of RA enlisted soldiers.

Projecting Regular Army Officers' Religious Affiliation

We now turn to the current and projected religious makeup of RA officers. Figure 3.20 illustrates the religious composition of RA officers over time. Panel A graphs the total number of officers in each religious category, and Panel B graphs these values as a percentage of the population. A substantial share of observations is missing information about religious affiliation; Panel C depicts the same percentages with these observations removed.

The religious composition of the RA officer population is considerably different than it is for the RA enlisted soldier population. Officers tend to be more likely to identify a religious affiliation than enlisted soldiers, with over 60 percent of officers identifying as Protestant, 30 percent identifying as Catholic, and fewer than 5 percent identifying as "None." The recent decline in the "None" population appears to be driven primarily by the rise in missing values. Both the Protestant and Catholic shares have remained relatively stable as a percentage of the officer population over time.

Figure 3.21 illustrates the percentage of RA officers in each religious family. Among officers, Catholics are the largest religious family, and they have experienced a relatively modest decline over time. Similar to enlisted soldiers, the Protestant—No Denomination group has increased substantially over the last two decades, while the percentage of officers in every other group appears to have experienced a slight downward trend. The share of "Nones" has declined substantially over time, although it is unclear whether this is driven by a true decrease in this category or a sudden increase in NA values amongst "None"

Figure 3.20
Religious Composition of RA Officers, FY 2000–2019

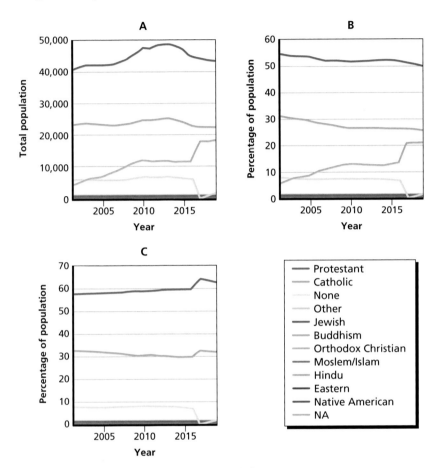

SOURCE: Author's calculations using TAPDB-AO data.
NOTE: The figure depicts the religious composition of RA officers using broad religious categories. Panel A presents the total number of officers in each category, Panel B presents these numbers as a percentage of the total population, and Panel C presents percentages with observations missing information on religious affiliation removed.

Figure 3.21
Proportion of RA Officers by Religious Family, FY 2000–2019

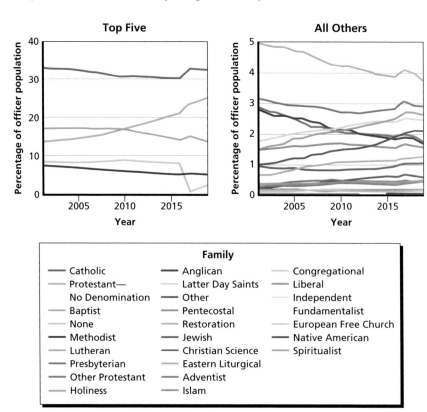

SOURCE: Author's calculations using TAPDB-AO data.

NOTE: Share of RA officers in each religious family over time. Because graphing all religious families at once creates a somewhat visually cluttered graph, we display the religions that account for the largest percentage of the population in the left panel, and the remaining religious (which make up less than 5 percent of the population) in the right panel. Colors in the legend are ordered by the ranking of each religion in the data using the percentage of the population when all years are pooled. Observations missing religious affiliation are excluded.

identifying officers (see Figure 3.20). The next-largest religious families are Baptists, Methodists, Lutherans, and Presbyterians. The most striking difference between the officer and enlisted soldier populations is the much smaller size of the "None" population and the larger percentage of Catholics amongst officers.

Next, we project the future religious composition of RA officers. Because Army officers are not recruited in the same way as enlisted soldiers, we do not consider the role of shifting geographic recruitment patterns in determining the future religious makeup of officers. Figure 3.22 illustrates the results of our forecasting model on RA officers. Because the religious composition of officers appears to be stable over time, we use simple linear regression to model the future religious composition.

Based on the results of our model, we expect the Protestant population to remain relatively stable or to increase by around 0.5 percentage points, Catholics to decrease by approximately 2 percentage points, and "Nones" to increase by approximately 1 percentage point, although the prediction interval on "Nones" is considerably larger than the other categories (indicating that there may be considerable variation in the future observed values of this group). In general, these results suggest that the RA officer population will maintain a fairly stable religious composition over time.

Figure 3.22
Forecasting the Religious Composition of RA Officers

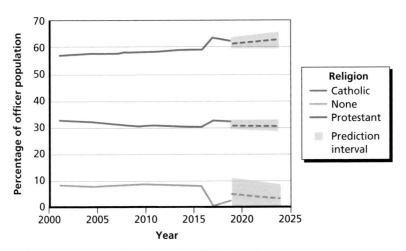

SOURCE: Author's own calculations using TAPDB-AO data.
NOTE: The figure shows the current proportions of the three largest religious groups using solid lines, and the projected proportions using dashed lines. The gray boxes illustrate 95-percent prediction intervals.

Figure 3.23
Forecasting the Religious Composition of Enlisted RA Soldiers and Officers

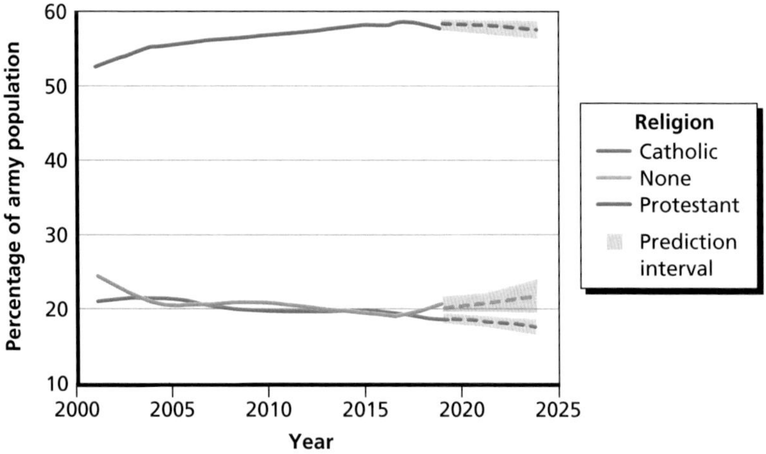

SOURCE: Author's calculations using both TAPDB-AE and TAPDB-AO data.
NOTE: The figure shows the current proportions of the three largest religious groups using solid lines, and the projected proportions using dashed lines. The gray boxes illustrate 95-percent prediction intervals.

Finally, we make a projection for the combined enlisted RA soldier and officer populations in Figure 3.23. Because chaplains serve both groups, this serves as an illustration of what the RA's religious composition could look like in the next five years. Pooling the two datasets shifts the curves substantially; while Protestants remain the largest religious group, the "None" and Catholic groups are much closer together. In keeping with the enlisted RA soldier projections, the "None" category remains larger than the Catholic category (this is to be expected because the officer population is considerably smaller than the enlisted soldier population).

Understanding Religious "Nones"

In all enlisted RA recruitment scenarios, individuals in the "None" category experience the largest increase as a proportion of the population.

This mirrors shifting trends in the religious composition of the United States as a whole; in recent years, the population of people who are religiously unaffiliated, along with those who identify as atheist and agnostic, has risen substantially. In the GSS, "Nones" have increased from 14 percent in 2000 to just over 23 percent in 2018. A 2019 study by the Pew Research Center further estimates that the "Nones" have increased to 26 percent of the U.S. population (Smith Schiller, and Nolan, 2019). The same study found that attendance at religious services has declined substantially in the last decade, with those who occasionally attend religious services now outnumbering those who attend more frequently (a reversal of the previous trend). These trends are even more concentrated among young people (who make up a substantial proportion of eligible Army recruits); while the GSS estimates that approximately 37 percent of Americans ages 18–24 identify as religious "Nones," Pew estimates that as many as 40 percent of millennials affiliate with this category. Overall, trends suggest that the U.S. population may be becoming more "secular" or nonreligious over time.

Does this mean that demand for chaplaincy services in the Army is decreasing? Surprisingly, evidence suggests that this is not necessarily the case. Although members of the "None" category in the United States typically choose not to identify with a traditional religious group, many hold theistic beliefs, have faith in an afterlife, and exhibit other characteristics that are typically associated with members of organized religious groups (Smith and Cragun, 2019). A number of studies have confirmed these conclusions (e.g., Hout and Fisher, 2002; Stark, 2008). Additionally, members of the "None" group may not necessarily be religious or identify with any organized religion, but spirituality may be an important component of their lives. For example, Pew finds that the percent of the population that identifies as "spiritual but not religious" increased from 19 to 27 percent of the U.S. population between 2012 and 2017 (Lipka and Gecewicz, 2017). Individuals who identify as "spiritual" may still believe in a higher power or in the transcendent, their spirituality may be an important guiding force for their decisions and their morality, and they may rely on their spirituality or a spiritual community for social support (e.g., Underwood and Teresi, 2002; Ammerman, 2013). Unlike someone who is expressly religious, a spiritual person may derive their sense of spirituality from a deity or theistic source, from their community or individualism, or from nature or the world around them. Whether someone is religious and spiritual, spiritual but not religious, or somewhere in the middle, they may still benefit from religious and spiritual support.

Another reason to suspect that "Nones" may still have religious or spiritual needs is that some studies of the U.S. population have found that membership in the "None" category is reasonably unstable over time. Using a representative survey of Americans and their religious beliefs over time, a study by Lim, MacGregor, and Putnam (2010) found that more than 30 percent of individuals who identified as religious "Nones" in one year identified with a religious group the following year. A similar percentage of respondents who identified with a religion the first year were in the "None" category the second year. The authors call these unstable "Nones," or "Liminal Nones," because this group is more religious than individuals who always identify in the "None" category, but less religious than those who always identify with a religious affiliation. "Liminal Nones" are therefore at the "margin of their religions, which they feel some attachment to and get involved in occasionally, but their connections are not strong enough to make them consistently identify with the religion." If the Army mirrors patterns in the broader American population to some extent, it is likely that many members of the "None" category in the TAPDB data would also fall into this group. It is important to note that the religious affiliation of soldiers is not continually or reliably updated over time; because of this, we are not able to measure the true percentage of soldiers who switch into or out of the "None" category.

There are a few Army-specific possibilities that may explain why the "None" category is on the rise (and some that may explain the rise in observations that are missing religious affiliation information altogether). First, the religious affiliation variable in the TAPDB administrative data relies on self-reporting by soldiers and is typically only filled out when a soldier initially enlists or when he or she receives new dog tags. Some soldiers may hurriedly check a "None" box (or may not check any box) by mistake, and they may not have a chance to update their response later. Second, a soldier may be religious but uninterested in participating in the religious services for a denomination; alternatively, the soldier may be unsure or in the process of changing religions at the time of enlistment. "None" may seem like a more flexible option to many soldiers. Lastly, as discussed above, a soldier may not identify strongly with a particular religion but may still be spiritual or have needs that can be met by DACH outside the boundaries of a denomination. For these reasons, soldiers who identify with the "None" category might still utilize chaplains' services and should not necessarily be considered secular or nonreligious. This may particularly be the case when we consider the breakdown of the "None" category by more detailed designations: More than 96 percent of soldiers who are counted in the "None" category identify as having "no religious preference," which is distinct from identifying as an atheist or an agnostic. This category is somewhat ambiguous, and there may be considerable variation in the spiritual needs of soldiers who choose not to identify any religious preference.

We investigate the percentage of individuals in the "None" category who are spiritual or would potentially benefit from having access to religious and spiritual services. Although the TAPDB does not provide information on soldiers' beliefs, we can infer this information from the GSS. To do so, we construct our own "spirituality" variable from GSS data. As described in Chapter Two, this variable takes on a value of one if a respondent reports believing in a higher power of some kind, that he or she is "slightly spiritual," or that he or she participates in religious or spiritual activities more often than "never." Similarly, we create a "moderately spiritual" variable that takes on a value of one if a person reports believing in a God more often than "sometimes," that he or she is at least "moderately" spiritual, or if he or she participates in religious activities at least multiple times a year. We focus on respondents' spirituality rather than their religiousness because these spiritual categories are fairly comprehensive and likely capture individuals with a broad range of religious and spiritual preferences; focusing just on "religiousness" would likely leave out some individuals who would also potentially benefit from DACH services.

Figure 3.24 shows the percentage of individuals in the "None" category in the GSS who meet the minimum threshold of spirituality,

Figure 3.24
Percentage of Americans Who Report No Religious Affiliation but Are Spiritual

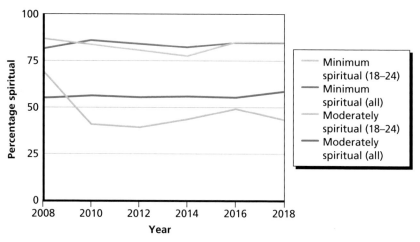

SOURCE: Author's calculations using data from GSS, undated.
NOTE: Percentage of respondents in the "None" category who meet the minimum spirituality threshold and the moderate spirituality threshold. The light-colored lines graph the same measures for the 18–24-year-old population.

and those who are at least moderately spiritual. We show this information both for the U.S. population and for people ages 18–24 (to reflect the age distribution of potential enlisted soldiers more closely). For both groups, the spiritual percentages are quite high: On average, around 84 percent of people in the U.S. who identify their religious affiliation as "None" are at least "minimally spiritual" or participate in religious activities more often than never. The 18–24 age group is similar; this group experiences a slight decline in spirituality between 2008 and 2014 but converges with the broader U.S. population by the end of the study period. On average, 83 percent of individuals in this age group in the "None" category meet a minimum spirituality threshold.

Around 55 percent of the "None" population consistently reports being at least moderately spiritual; among the 18–24 age group, the share is somewhat lower (approximately 45 percent). The younger demographic also experiences more variation over time, with the moderately spiritual group initially decreasing in 2008, followed by moderate gains and another decline after 2016. If this pattern is similar among soldiers, it suggests that a fairly large proportion of people who report that they do not identify with a religion may still utilize chaplaincy services or benefit from support from DACH.

Figure 3.25 extrapolates these findings to the enlisted RA soldier population and compares the projected change in the religious "None" population among enlisted RA soldiers to the estimated population of "Nones" who are likely to be spiritual. To make this estimate, we used the average spiritual percentage from the 18–24-year-old population in the GSS and multiplied it by the proportion of "Nones" in the enlisted RA population (we use the Scenario 1 projection here, but the analysis could be repeated for all scenarios). As the proportion of "Nones" in the RA approaches 25 percent, we expect that close to 20 percent of soldiers will identify as "None" but meet our minimum threshold of spirituality, while 10 percent will identify as "None" but meet the

Figure 3.25
Estimated Percentage of Enlisted RA Soldiers Reporting No Religious Affiliation Who May Be Spiritual

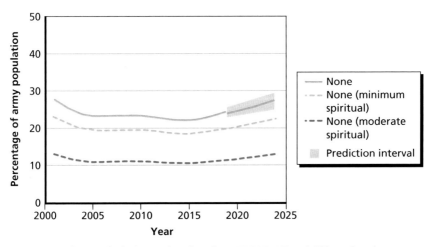

SOURCE: Author's calculations using data from TAPDB-AE and GSS, undated.
NOTE: The figure shows the current and projected (Scenario 1) proportion of enlisted RA soldiers in the "None" category (gray solid line), as well as the percentage of those soldiers predicted to be at least minimally spiritual (light-red dashed line), and the percentage predicted to be at least moderately spiritual (dark-red dashed line).

threshold for moderate spirituality. Again, this suggests that, while the proportion of individuals in the "None" category is on the rise, many members of this group may still wish to participate in spiritual or religious activities, although they may not identify with a particular religion or denomination.

CHAPTER FOUR

Conclusions

In this report, we used administrative TAPDB data on enlisted RA soldiers and officers and GSS data on the U.S. population to study trends in religious composition over time. In particular, we addressed the following questions:

How Has the Religious Composition of Enlisted Regular Army Soldiers Changed over Time?

The three largest groups in the enlisted RA are Protestants, Catholics, and "Nones." The proportion of Protestants has increased over time, while the proportion of Catholics has fallen slightly, and the proportion of "Nones" has been relatively stable. These patterns are largely driven by the religious composition of soldiers coming from the southern United States, who make up nearly half the enlisted soldier population. By breaking down these religious groups by more detailed religious families, we find that, within Protestants, nondenominational Protestants are growing substantially, while most other denominational families have declined in recent years. Future research is needed to better understand what the rise of "nondenominational" Protestants means for the religious and spiritual needs of soldiers and the role of DACH in their religious lives.

How Does the Religious Composition of the U.S. Population Compare with the Religious Composition of the Enlisted Regular Army?

Comparing RA enlisted soldiers to the U.S. population, we find that, while Protestants are the largest group overall in both populations, the proportion of Protestants is increasing among RA enlisted soldiers while it is simultaneously decreasing in the United States. The United States also has a larger proportion of Catholics than are found among enlisted soldiers. While enlisted soldiers initially had a larger proportion of "Nones," the shares of "Nones" among the enlisted soldier population and the U.S. population have converged over time. We also compare the enlisted RA population to the population in the GSS with the same age and regional composition (which roughly approximates the youth cohort from the same parts of the country as enlisted RA soldiers); this weighted transformation shows that the enlisted RA population is substantially different from the broader population from which it is recruited. Based on the GSS data, we would expect the enlisted RA population to have fewer Protestants, more Catholics, and more individuals in the "None" category than there are currently. The enlisted RA population is, therefore, substantially different from both the U.S. youth cohort and the broader U.S. population.

How Does the Religious Composition of Regular Army Chaplains Compare with the Religious Composition of Enlisted Regular Army Soldiers?

The top two religious groups represented by RA chaplains are Protestants and Catholics. There are roughly six Protestant chaplains for every 1,000 enlisted RA soldiers, and about one Catholic chaplain per 1,000 Catholic enlisted RA soldiers. At least for Catholics, however, the ratio of Catholic chaplains to soldiers is twice the ratio of Catholic priests to Catholics in the civilian population. While the number of chaplains in other religious categories is relatively small, smaller religious groups tend to have more chaplains for every 1,000 soldiers (e.g., there are currently 12 chaplains for every 1,000 Orthodox Christian soldiers). There are also considerable differences in the representation of religious families among the chaplains, compared with the composition of religious families among soldiers. While "nondenominational" Protestants are on the rise among enlisted soldiers, Baptists, Presbyterians, Pentecostals, and Methodists are among the largest religious families represented by the chaplains.

What Is the Likely Projected Religious Composition in the Enlisted Regular Army over the Next Five Years?

We answer this question by making five-year projections of the three major religious groups using second-degree polynomial regression. Based on the current geographic makeup of the enlisted RA, our projections suggest that the share of Protestants will decline modestly, the share of "Nones" will increase, and the share of Catholics will decrease.

How Might These Projections Shift If the Army Increases Recruitment from Currently Underrepresented Regions in the United States?

We answer this question using two different scenarios: In one scenario (Scenario 2), we assume that the Army shifts its geographic recruitment patterns but that doing so does not cause any religious groups to become more or less likely to enlist. We predict that this would cause a slight decrease in Protestants, relative to the baseline scenario in which current trends continue (Scenario 1), and a slight increase in Catholics and "Nones." Another scenario (Scenario 3) assumes that shifting geographic recruitment patterns induces the religious composition of enlisted soldiers to become more similar to the religious composition of the United States. In this scenario, there is a larger decline in the share of Protestants, and a larger increase in the share of "Nones." The share of Catholics increases at first, mirroring the much higher proportion of Catholics in the U.S. population. However, the proportion of Catholics ultimately declines over time, and trends in the data suggest that Catholics will continue to decline as a percentage of the RA population under this scenario.

How Has the Religious Composition of Regular Army Officers Changed over Time, and What Is the Likely Projected Religious Composition of Regular Army Officers over the Next Five Years?

RA officers tend to be more religious than the enlisted population, with the "None" population making up less than 5 percent. Based on trends in the data and our projections, we expect the religious composition of the officer population to remain relatively stable over the next five years.

What Can We Learn About the Spiritual Needs of Individuals Who Report Not Having a Religious Affiliation?

Using the GSS data, we find that a sizeable proportion of individuals (~83 percent) who identify with the "None" category are still somewhat spiritual (at minimum), while nearly 50 percent are moderately spiritual. Based on this, we conclude that a large number of soldiers in the "None" category may still benefit from DACH services.

Supplementary Figures and Tables

This appendix includes supplementary figures. Figure A.1 shows the total population of enlisted RA soldiers in each religious category over time, compared with RA soldiers by recruit year. This comparison is shown to highlight one of the primary reasons that we chose to project the data by the total population, rather than by recruits: While the number of Army recruits varies dramatically by year, total enlisted RA soldiers are a much more stable population. As such, we felt that projections based on total soldiers would be a more plausible representation of how the Army's religious composition might change in years to come.

The following three figures compare the TAPDB-AE data and GSS data by a number of important variables. Figure A.2 compares the regional distribution of the RA to respondents in the GSS. The regional composition of each dataset is fairly similar, with the South making up the largest population, followed by the West and Midwest, and the Northeast representing the smallest proportion of the population. The Army soldiers, however, are much more heavily concentrated in the South than the sample from the GSS. Figure A.3 compares the age distribution of both datasets, and Figure A.4 compares the distribution of the data by gender. Soldiers in the TAPDB-AE data typically belong to the 18–24 and 25–34 age group, a smaller proportion are between 35 and 44 years of age, and close to 0 percent are 45 or older. Close to 20 percent of GSS respondents are between the ages of 25 and 65, while comparatively fewer respondents are very young (18–24) or old (65 or older). The composition of the RA soldiers and GSS respondents by gender is also considerably different. In any given

Figure A.1
Religious Composition of Enlisted RA Population (All Years) Compared with the Enlisted RA Population (Recruit Years)

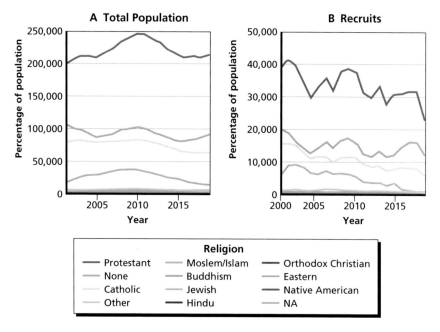

SOURCE: TAPDB-AE and author's calculations.
NOTE: The figure shows the total number of enlisted RA soldiers in each religious category by year. Panel A shows it for soldiers serving in all years, while Panel B shows it for soldiers by the year they were recruited.

year, the makeup of RA soldiers is typically 85 percent male and 15 percent female. By comparison, around 45 percent of GSS respondents are male, and 55 percent are female.

Figure A.5 shows the geographically weighted and gender-weighted GSS data (compared with the TAPDB-AE data) that was used to create the projected values for Scenario 3. Since there are significant differences between the religiosity of men and women, the GSS data is weighted by proportions of each gender in the RA population (0.85 men and 0.15 women) to better represent the underlying population from which the Army is recruited. The sample is also limited to individuals younger than 55. Sample sizes in the GSS are particularly

Figure A.2
Regional Distribution of RA Enlisted Soldiers Compared with the
Regional Distribution of GSS Respondents

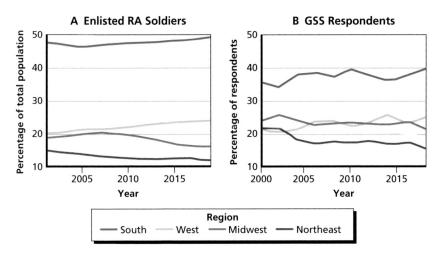

SOURCE: TAPDB-AE, GSS, and author's calculations

NOTE: The graph depicts the percentage of enlisted RA soldiers by region of permanent residence in Panel A compared with the percentage of GSS respondents by region of residence in Panel B.

small for some age groups, and may not be a full representation of the religious preferences of those groups; as a result, we chose not to weight the GSS data by age when making the projections, and we instead chose to remove older respondents from the calculation (as individuals in this category are least likely to be members of the RA).

Figures A.6 and A.7 provide a breakdown of the three GSS variables that were used to make the spiritual variables in the analysis of those reporting no religious affiliation ("Nones"). These variables were chosen based on relevance and data availability (many similar questions were asked inconsistently over time, or only in one year). Figure A.6 graphs each of the three variables over time, while Figure A.7 provides histograms of each variable to show the distribution of people in the "None" category across each possible response value. The variables have been recoded (where necessary) so that one is equal to "no" or "none" and the maximum value is equal to the strongest pos-

Figure A.3
Age Distribution of RA Enlisted Soldiers Compared with the
Age Distribution of GSS Respondents

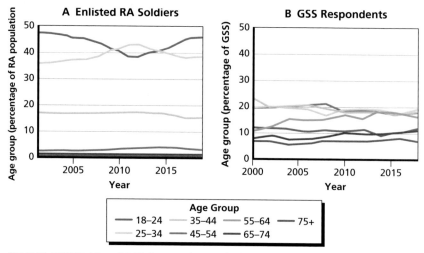

SOURCE: TAPDB-AE and GSS data, author's calculations

NOTE: The figure graphs the percentage of the RA enlisted soldiers and the GSS respondents in each age group.

Figure A.4
Gender Distribution of RA Enlisted Soldiers Compared with the
Gender Distribution of GSS Respondents

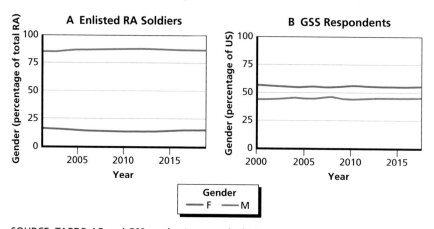

SOURCE: TAPDB-AE and GSS, author's own calculations.

NOTE: The figure depicts the percentage of the enlisted RA population and GSS respondents by reported gender.

Figure A.5
Geographically and Gender-Weighted TAPDB-AE and GSS Data

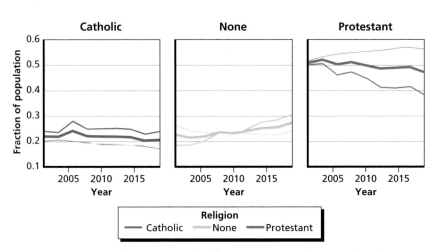

SOURCE: Author's calculations using data from TAPDB-AE and GSS, undated.

NOTE: Geographically and gender-weighted TAPDB-AE (light-colored line) and GSS (darker line) data. The average of these two values is the bold line in the middle of each plot. These average values were used to make projections for Scenario 3.

sible response (e.g., strong belief in God, frequent participation in religious activities, and very spiritual). Table A.1 details the thresholds that needed to be met in each variable to be classified as "spiritual" or "moderately spiritual."

Table A.1
Variable Thresholds for "Spiritual" Calculations

Spiritual Measure	Participation in Religious Activities	Considers Self a "Spiritual Person"	Belief in God
Minimum spiritual	>1 (no participation)	>1 (not spiritual)	>2 (no belief or not sure)
Moderately spiritual	4 or higher (at least a few times a year)	3 or higher (at least "moderately spiritual")	>4 (sometimes believes in God)

NOTE: The table lists the variable thresholds needed to be classified as somewhat (minimum) spiritual or moderately spiritual. A detailed breakdown of each variable can be found in Figures A.6 and A.7.

Figure A.6
Average Values of GSS Variables Used to Construct the Variable "Spiritual"

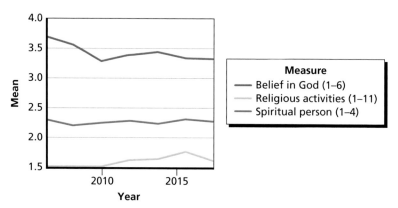

SOURCE: Author's calculations using data from GSS, undated.

NOTE: Average response value to each survey question from respondents in the GSS who reported "None" for religious affiliation. These questions were first asked in 2006 but were not asked consistently until 2008. As a result, we only use values from 2008 and later in our analysis.

Figure A.7
Histograms of Spiritual Variables

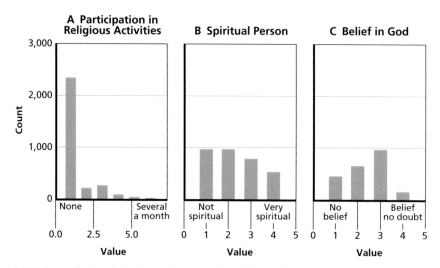

SOURCE: Author's calculations using data from GSS, undated.

NOTE: Histograms for each variable from the GSS. The histograms represent the distribution of responses by people who reported "None" for religious affiliation.

Figure A.8 compares religious composition in the TAPDB-AE with GSS data that have been weighted by region, age, and education level to match the distributions in the TAPDB-AE data. While the final weighted version incorporates region, age, and gender, education is another variable of interest that was also considered. Because most soldiers enlist after high school, weighting the GSS by education effectively narrows the population to respondents with a high school education or below. This weighted version of the GSS narrows the sample size of the GSS even more by weighting a fairly small proportion of the GSS respondents much more heavily than others. Thus, we chose not to include this figure in the main document. However, it is still an interesting comparison; even after adjusting for region, age, and education, there are still fairly clear differences between the two populations.

Figure A.8
Religious Composition Among Enlisted RA Soldiers and U.S. Population (Weighted by Region, Age, and Education)

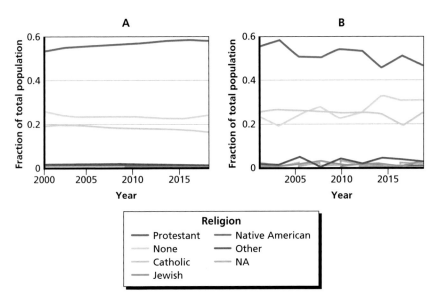

SOURCE: Author's calculations using data from TAPDB-AE and GSS, undated.

NOTE: Panel A shows the religious composition of enlisted RA soldiers from the TAPDB-AE data, while Panel B shows what the GSS religious composition looks like after being weighted by the region, age, and educational composition of the TAPDB-AE data.

Figures A.9 and A.10 show the graphs of religious family composition among enlisted soldiers and officers, respectively, without removing observations missing information about religious affiliation or state of permanent residence at the time of enlistment ("NA"). In both graphs, increasing NA values shifts the other curves down; in the main body of the text, we chose to remove these NA values because we have no way of knowing how they would impact our analysis if the data were available.

Figure A.9
Religious Family Composition of RA Enlisted Soldiers (Including Observations Missing Religious Affiliation Information)

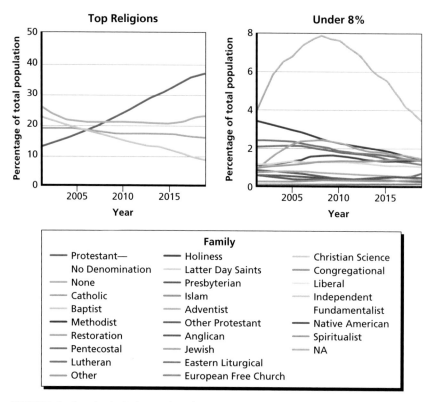

SOURCE: Authors' calculations using the TAPDB-AE and ARDA, undated.
NOTE: The graph shows the proportion of enlisted RA soldiers in each religious family. Observations missing information about religious information or state of permanent residence at the time of enlistment are included ("NA" line).

Figure A.10
Religious Family Composition of RA Officers (Including Observations Missing Religious Affiliation Information)

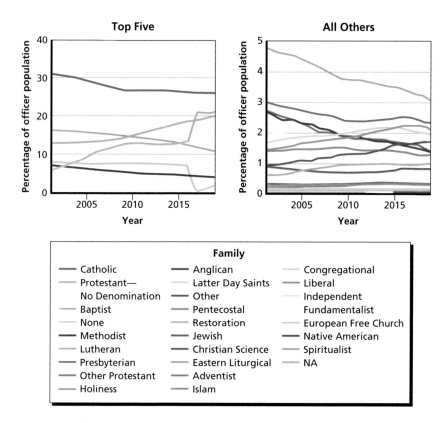

SOURCE: Authors' calculations using the TAPDB-AO and ARDA, undated.

NOTE: The graph shows the proportion of RA officers in each religious family. The top five families are presented in the first panel, while all other families are in the second. Observations missing information about religious information are included ("NA" line).

Finally, for reference, Table A.2 provides a much more detailed breakdown of the religious categories (GSS, undated) and families (ARDA, undated) that are used throughout the report. Because of the size of this table, we decided to include it in the appendix, rather than print it directly in the report.

Table A.2
Religious Groupings Based on the GSS and the ARDA

RELDEN	RELDEN_code (TAPDB)	Religious Group (GSS)	Family (ARDA)
14	buddhism	Buddhism	other
62	roman catholic church	Catholic	catholic
CC	catholic churches	Catholic	catholic
EQ	anglican catholic church	Catholic	catholic
13	christian, no denominational preference	Christian	protestant—no denomination
KK	eastern religions	Eastern	other
MA	sikh	Eastern	other
49	hindu	Hindu	other
36	jewish/judaism	Jewish	jewish
FA	reformed judaism	Jewish	jewish
FB	conservative judaism	Jewish	jewish
FC	orthodox judaism	Jewish	jewish
MJ	union messianic jewish congregations	Jewish	jewish
48	islam	Moslem/Islam	islam
0	no preference recorded	NA	NA
99	unknown	NA	NA
AQ	native american	Native American	native american
1	no religious preference	None	none
75	atheist	None	none
ZB	agnostic	None	none
53	eastern orthodox churches	Orthodox Christian	eastern liturgical
AN	antiochian orthodox christian	Orthodox Christian	eastern liturgical

Table A.2—Continued

RELDEN	RELDEN_code (TAPDB)	Religious Group (GSS)	Family (ARDA)
BA	anglican orthodox church, the	Orthodox Christian	anglican
MB	greek orthodox church	Orthodox Christian	eastern liturgical
OO	orthodox churches	Orthodox Christian	eastern liturgical
11	sacred well congregation	Other	other
73	wicca	Other	other
74	other religions	Other	other
AI	church of the spiral tree	Other	other
AP	the troth	Other	other
EA	eckankar	Other	other
HU	humanist	Other	other
KF	baha' i faith	Other	other
MC	rosicrucianism	Other	other
NG	a druid fellowship	Other	other
NH	deism	Other	other
XX	unclassified religions	Other	other
YY	magick and spiritualist	Other	other
2	seventh-day adventists	Protestant	adventist
4	assemblies of god	Protestant	pentecostal
5	grace gospel fellowship	Protestant	independent fundamentalist
6	american baptist churches	Protestant	baptist
7	independent baptist bible mission	Protestant	baptist
8	southern baptist convention	Protestant	baptist
9	national association of free will baptists	Protestant	baptist

Table A.2—Continued

RELDEN	RELDEN_code (TAPDB)	Religious Group (GSS)	Family (ARDA)
10	baptist churches, other	Protestant	baptist
12	brethren church	Protestant	european free church
16	christian science (first church of christ, scientist)	Protestant	christian science
18	church of christ	Protestant	holiness
19	church of god in christ	Protestant	pentecostal
20	church of god	Protestant	holiness
24	christian church (disciples of christ)	Protestant	restoration
26	protestant episcopal church	Protestant	anglican
32	friends (quaker)	Protestant	european free church
34	jehovahs witness	Protestant	adventist
38	church of jesus christ of latter	Protestant	latter day saints
40	lutheran churches	Protestant	lutheran
41	lutheran council in the usa	Protestant	lutheran
44	methodist churches	Protestant	methodist
45	evangelical church of north america	Protestant	holiness
46	evangelical covenant church in america	Protestant	methodist
47	evangelical church alliance, the	Protestant	independent fundamentalist
50	church of the nazarene	Protestant	holiness
55	full gospel pentecostal association, the	Protestant	pentecostal
56	pentecostal churches	Protestant	pentecostal
57	united pentecostal church, international	Protestant	pentecostal
58	presbyterian churches	Protestant	presbyterian
60	reformed churches	Protestant	presbyterian

Table A.2—Continued

RELDEN	RELDEN_code (TAPDB)	Religious Group (GSS)	Family (ARDA)
64	salvation army, the	Protestant	holiness
66	unitarian universalist association	Protestant	liberal
68	united church of christ	Protestant	congregational
70	protestant—other churches	Protestant	other protestant
72	protestant—no denominational preference	Protestant	protestant—no denomination
A0	american council christian church	Protestant	other protestant
AA	asbury bible churches	Protestant	other protestant
AB	bible protestant church	Protestant	other protestant
AC	congregational methodist church	Protestant	methodist
AD	evangelical methodist church of america	Protestant	methodist
AE	fundamental methodist church, inc.	Protestant	methodist
AF	independent churches affiliated	Protestant	other protestant
AG	independent fundamental bible churches	Protestant	independent fundamentalist
AH	tioga river christian conference	Protestant	other protestant
AJ	ukrainian evangelical baptist conference	Protestant	baptist
AK	methodist protestant church	Protestant	methodist
AL	militant fundamental bible churches	Protestant	other protestant
AM	united christian church	Protestant	methodist
AO	anglican church in america	Protestant	anglican
AV	adventist churches	Protestant	adventist
B0	associated gospel churches, the	Protestant	other protestant
BB	baptist bible fellowship	Protestant	baptist
BC	brethren in christ fellowship	Protestant	european free church
BD	christian crusade	Protestant	other protestant

Table A.2—Continued

RELDEN	RELDEN_code (TAPDB)	Religious Group (GSS)	Family (ARDA)
BE	independent baptist churches	Protestant	baptist
BF	independent lutheran churches	Protestant	lutheran
BG	southwide baptist fellowship	Protestant	baptist
BH	bible presbyterian church	Protestant	presbyterian
BT	american baptist conference	Protestant	baptist
CA	american baptist association	Protestant	baptist
CB	cooperative baptist fellowship, inc	Protestant	Baptist
CD	baptist missionary association of america	Protestant	Baptist
CE	free will baptists	Protestant	Baptist
CF	general association of general baptists	Protestant	Baptist
CG	general association of regular baptist churches	Protestant	Baptist
CH	american baptist convention	Protestant	Baptist
CI	american baptist churches in usa	Protestant	Baptist
CJ	world baptist fellowship	Protestant	Baptist
DA	advent christian church	Protestant	adventist
DB	african methodist episcopal church	Protestant	methodist
DC	african methodist episcopal zion church	Protestant	methodist
DD	baptist general conference	Protestant	Baptist
DE	christian methodist episcopal church	Protestant	methodist
DF	christian reformed church	Protestant	presbyterian
DG	church of god (anderson, in)	Protestant	holiness
DH	church of god in north america	Protestant	holiness
DJ	evangelical congregational church	Protestant	methodist
DK	baptist general convention of texas	Protestant	Baptist

Table A.2—Continued

RELDEN	RELDEN_code (TAPDB)	Religious Group (GSS)	Family (ARDA)
DL	free will baptists, nc state convention of	Protestant	Baptist
DM	moravian church	Protestant	methodist
DN	national association of congregational christian churches	Protestant	congregational
DP	national baptist convention of america	Protestant	Baptist
DQ	national baptist convention, usa, inc.	Protestant	Baptist
DR	north american baptist conference	Protestant	Baptist
DS	primitive methodist church, usa	Protestant	methodist
DT	progressive national baptist convention, inc	Protestant	baptist
DU	reformed church in america	Protestant	presbyterian
DV	church of god general conference	Protestant	adventist
DW	seventh day baptist general conference	Protestant	Baptist
DX	churches of god, general conference	Protestant	presbyterian
DY	schwenkfelder churches, the general conference of	Protestant	european free church
DZ	the swedenborgian church, general conference of	Protestant	spiritualist
EC	episcopal church	Protestant	anglican
ED	church of god in prophecy	Protestant	pentecostal
EE	episcopal churches	Protestant	anglican
EH	bible churches chaplaincy	Protestant	pentecostal
EI	chaplaincy full gospel churches (cfgc)	Protestant	pentecostal
EJ	fellowship of grace brethren churches	Protestant	european free church
EK	plymouth brethren	Protestant	independent fundamentalist
EL	reformed church in the united states	Protestant	presbyterian

Table A.2—Continued

RELDEN	RELDEN_code (TAPDB)	Religious Group (GSS)	Family (ARDA)
EM	reformed episcopal church	Protestant	anglican
EN	reorganized church of jesus christ of latter day saints	Protestant	latter day saints
EP	churches of christ	Protestant	restoration
FF	fundamentalist churches	Protestant	independent fundamentalist
GA	lutheran church in america	Protestant	lutheran
GB	american lutheran church, the	Protestant	lutheran
GC	lutheran church	Protestant	lutheran
GD	evangelical lutheran churches, association of	Protestant	lutheran
GG	restoration churches	Protestant	restoration
HH	holiness churches	Protestant	holiness
JA	christian and missionary alliance	Protestant	holiness
JB	christian churches and churches of Christ	Protestant	restoration
JC	church of god (cleveland, tn)	Protestant	pentecostal
JD	church of the united brethren in christ	Protestant	methodist
JE	churches of christ in christian union	Protestant	holiness
JF	conservative baptist association of america	Protestant	Baptist
JG	conservative congregational christian conference	Protestant	presbyterian
JH	elim fellowship	Protestant	pentecostal
JJ	evangelical free church of america	Protestant	methodist
JK	evangelical friends alliance	Protestant	european free church
JL	evangelical methodist church	Protestant	methodist
JM	international church of the foursquare gospel	Protestant	pentecostal

Table A.2—Continued

RELDEN	RELDEN_code (TAPDB)	Religious Group (GSS)	Family (ARDA)
JN	open bible standard churches, inc.	Protestant	pentecostal
JO	national association of evangelicals	Protestant	holiness
JP	pentecostal churches of god of america, inc	Protestant	pentecostal
JQ	pentecostal holiness church	Protestant	pentecostal
JR	missionary church, the	Protestant	holiness
JS	general conference of the brethren church	Protestant	european free church
JT	central bible church	Protestant	other protestant
JU	free lutheran congregation	Protestant	lutheran
JV	elim missionary assemblies	Protestant	pentecostal
JW	kansas yearly meeting of friends	Protestant	european free church
JX	missionary church association	Protestant	holiness
JY	ohio yearly meeting of friends	Protestant	european free church
JZ	korean evangelical church of america	Protestant	presbyterian
LA	associate reformed presbyterian church	Protestant	presbyterian
LB	cumberland presbyterian church	Protestant	presbyterian
LC	presbyterian church in the united states	Protestant	presbyterian
LD	united presbyterian church, evangelical synod	Protestant	presbyterian
LE	orthodox presbyterian church, the	Protestant	presbyterian
LF	reformed presbyterian church, evangelical synod	Protestant	presbyterian
LG	united presbyterian church in the usa	Protestant	presbyterian
LH	presbyterian church in america	Protestant	presbyterian
LJ	presbyterian council for chaplains and military personnel	Protestant	presbyterian

Table A.2—Continued

RELDEN	RELDEN_code (TAPDB)	Religious Group (GSS)	Family (ARDA)
NB	free methodist church of north america	Protestant	holiness
NC	primitive methodist church, the	Protestant	methodist
ND	the wesleyan church	Protestant	holiness
NE	southern methodist church	Protestant	methodist
NF	united methodist church, the	Protestant	methodist
QQ	european free churches	Protestant	european free church
VV	evangelical churches	Protestant	other protestant
XC	iglesia ni christo	Protestant	liberal
XJ	churches of the new jerusalem	Protestant	spiritualist
XN	new age churches	Protestant	other

NOTES: This table provides an exhaustive list of the detailed religious designations provided by the TAPDB administrative data, and the groupings based on the GSS and ARDA categorizations. Categories were defined by each organization, and the grouping was conducted manually by the author. The RELDEN code is the unique code used by the Army administrative data (TAPDB) to categorize each religious denomination.

References

Ammerman, N. T., "Spiritual but Not Religious? Beyond Binary Choices in the Study of Religion," *Journal for the Scientific Study of Religion*, Vol. 52, 2013, pp. 258–278.

ARDA—*See* Association of Religion Data Archives.

Association of Religion Data Archives, "Religious Groups: Profiles," webpage, undated. As of September 4, 2020:
http://www.thearda.com/denoms/families/groups.asp

Center for Applied Research in the Apostolate, "Frequently Requested Church Statistics," webpage, undated. As of November 17, 2020:
https://cara.georgetown.edu/frequently-requested-church-statistics/

DODM—*See* U.S. Department of Defense Manual.

General Social Survey, homepage, undated. As of September 4, 2020:
https://gss.norc.org/

GSS—*See* General Social Survey.

Hout, M., and C. Fischer, "Why More Americans Have No Religious Preference: Politics and Generations," *American Sociological Review*, Vol. 67, No. 2, 2002, pp. 165–190.

Lim, C., C. A. MacGregor, and R. D. Putnam, "Secular and Liminal: Discovering Heterogeneity Among Religious Nones," *Journal for the Scientific Study of Religion*, Vol. 49, 2010, pp. 596–618.

Lipka, M., and C. Gecewicz, "More Americans Now Say They're Spiritual but Not Religious," Pew Research Center, September 6, 2017. As of February 1, 2021:
https://www.pewresearch.org/fact-tank/2017/09/06/more-americans-now-say
-theyre-spiritual-but-not-religious/

Mead, F. S., S. S. Hill, and C. D. Atwood, *Handbook of Denominations in the United States*, 12th ed., Nashville, Tenn.: Abingdon Press, 2005.

Melton, G. J., *Encyclopedia of American Religions*, Farmington Hills, Mich.: The Gale Group, Inc., 2003.

Miles, F., "Army Stepping Up Recruitment in 22 Left-Leaning Cities," Fox News, January 2, 2019. As of September 4, 2020:
https://www.foxnews.com/us/army-stepping-up-recruitment-in-22-left-leaning -cities

Pew Research Center, "America's Changing Religious Landscape," webpage, May 12, 2015. As of March 29, 2021:
https://www.pewforum.org/2015/05/12/americas-changing-religious-landscape/

Philipps, D., "The Army, in Need of Recruits, Turns Focus to Liberal-Leaning Cities," *New York Times*, January 2, 2019. As of September 4, 2020:
https://www.nytimes.com/2019/01/02/us/army-recruiting-tech-industry-seattle .html

Reid, G., R. D. Linder, B. L. Shelley, and H. S. Stout, eds., *Dictionary of Christianity in America*, Downers Grove, Ill.: InterVarsity Press, 1990.

Smith, J. M., and R. T. Cragun, "Mapping Religion's Other: A Review of the Study of Nonreligion and Secularity," *Journal for the Scientific Study of Religion*, Vol. 58, 2019, pp. 319–335.

Smith, G. A., A. Schiller, and H. Nolan, "In U.S., Decline of Christianity Continues at Rapid Pace," Pew Research Center, October 17, 2019. February 1, 2021:
https://www.pewforum.org/2019/10/17/in-u-s-decline-of-christianity-continues -at-rapid-pace/

Smith, T. W., M. Davern, J. Freese, and S. Morgan, "General Social Surveys," 1972–2018, Data accessed from the GSS Data Explorer website at gssdataexplorer .norc.org

Stark, R., *What Americans Really Believe: New Findings from the Baylor Surveys of Religion*, Waco, Tex.: Baylor University Press, 2008.

Steensland, B., J. Park, M. Regnerus, L. Robinson, W. Wilcox, and R. Woodberry, "The Measure of American Religion: Toward Improving the State of the Art," *Social Forces*, Vol. 79, No. 1, 2000, pp. 291–318.

Stetzer, E., and R. Burge, "Reltrad Coding Problems and a New Repository," *Politics and Religion*, Vol. 9, No. 1, 2016, pp. 187–190.

Underwood, L. G., and J. A. Teresi, "The Daily Spiritual Experience Scale: Development, Theoretical Description, Reliability, Exploratory Factor Analysis, and Preliminary Construct Validity Using Health-Related Data," *Annals of Behavioral Medicine*, Vol. 24, No. 1, 1972–2018, pp. 22–33. https://doi.org/10.1207/S15324796ABM2401_04

United States Army Human Resources Command (HRC), "Total Army Personnel Database Active Enlisted Soldiers," 2019.

United States Army Human Resources Command (HRC), "Total Army Personnel Database Active Officers," 2019.

U.S. Census Bureau, "Annual Estimates of the Resident Population for the United States, Regions, States, and Puerto Rico: April 1, 2010 to July 1, 2018," 2018. As of February 1, 2021:
https://www.census.gov/newsroom/press-kits/2018/pop-estimates-national-state.html.

U.S. Census Bureau, *Census Regions and Divisions of the United States*, webpage, 2010. As of September 4, 2020:
https://www.census.gov/geographies/reference-maps/2010/geo/2010-census-regions-and-divisions-of-the-united-states.html

U.S. Department of Defense Manual 7730.54, "Reserve Components Common Personnel Data System (RCCPDS): Reporting Procedures," Incorporating Change 2, January 28, 2019.

Wiederaenders, R. C., ed., *Historical Guide to Lutheran Church Bodies in North America*, St. Louis, Mo.: Lutheran Historical Conference, 1998.